BALM IN GILEAD

BY LANFORD WILSON

★

★

DRAMATISTS
PLAY SERVICE
INC.

To Tanya

Balm in Gilead was first produced by Cafe La MaMa Experimental Theatre Club, (Ellen Stewart, Artistic Director) in New York City, on January 26, 1965. It was directed by Marshall W. Mason; the lighting design was by Dennis Parichy; and the stage manager was Lola Richardson. The cast was as follows:

JOHN	Marvin Alexander
ERNESTO	Thomas Ambrosio
CARLO	Howard Benson
BABE	Savannah Bentley
RUST	Claris Erickson
BONNIE	Linda Eskenas
FICK	Neil Flanagan
FRANNY	Frank Geraci
DAVID	Gary Gusick
TIG	Paul Kilb
RAKE	John Kramer
MARTIN	Matthew Lewis
BOB	Harry McCormick
FRANK, AL	Jerry Newman
DARLENE	Avra Petrides
DOPEY	Michael Warren Powell
KAY	Barbara Randolph
JOE	Gregory Rozakis
TERRY	Lucy Silvay
ANN	Mary Tahmin
XAVIER	Dennis Tate
STRANGER	Robert Thirkield
TIM	Ronald Willoughby
JUDY	Phoebe Wray

Balm in Gilead was produced by Steppenwolf Theatre Company at the Steppenwolf Theatre in Chicago, Illinois, on September 18, 1980. It was directed by John Malkovich; the set and lighting designs were by Kevin Rigdon; and the stage manager was Terri McClure. The case was as follows:

JOHN .... John Mahoney
ERNESTO .... Kim Nardelli
CARLO .... Paul Jones
BABE .... Debra Engle
RUST .... Billie Williams
BONNIE .... Rondi Reed
FICK .... Terry Kinney
FRANNY .... Jeff Perry
DAVID .... Doug Gould
TIG .... William L. Petersen
RAKE .... Alan Wilder
MARTIN .... Rick Snyder
BOB .... Robert Biggs
FRANK .... Bill Williams
AL .... Michael Moore
DARLENE .... Laurie Metcalf
DOPEY .... Gary Sinise
KAY .... Kathi O'Donnell
JOE .... Francis Guinan
TERRY .... Michelle Banks
ANN .... Glenne Headly
XAVIER .... Tom Zanarini
STRANGER .... Tom Irwin
TIM .... Randy Amov
JUDY .... Joan Allen
CHILDREN .... Aaron, Dylan, and Greg Kramer

Balm in Gilead was produced by Circle Repertory Company and Steppenwolf Theatre Company at Circle Repertory in New York City, on May 15,1984. The production then transferred to the Minetta Lane Theatre, where it opened on September 6, 1984. It was directed by John Malkovich; the set and lighting designs were by Kevin Rigdon. The case was as follows:

JOHN .... Paul Butler
ERNESTO .... Giancarlo Esposito
CARLO .... Lazaro Perez
BABE .... Debra Engle
RUST .... Billie Neal
BONNIE .... Tanya Berezin
FICK .... Terry Kinney
FRANNY .... Jeff Perry
DAVID .... Brian Tarantina
TIG .... James McDaniel
RAKE .... James Picken, Jr.
MARTIN .... Jonathan Hogan
BOB .... Bruce McCarty
FRANK .... Zane Lasky
AL .... Burke Pearson
DARLENE .... Laurie Metcalf
DOPEY .... Gary Sinise
KAY .... Betsy Aidem
JOE .... Danton Stone
TERRY .... Karen Sederholm
ANN .... Glenne Headly
XAVIER .... Tom Zanarini
STRANGER .... Tom Irwin
TIM .... Mick Weber
JUDY .... Charlotte Maier
CHILDREN .... Adam Davidson, Eben Davidson,
Erinnisse Heuer, and Samantha Kostmayer

NOTES

SCENE: An all-night coffee shop and the street corner outside. Upper Broadway, New York City.

The café is represented, or suggested, in the center of a wide, high stage. There are a counter and stools (one unit) and across a wide aisle, a row of booths (one unit). They should be constructed so the actors can raise and move them easily. There is also some indication of an area behind the counter; and a skeletal indication of a front door and large front window.

Actors wander onto the set from both sides and back; they gather in the café and outside, where the street corner would be (downstage left). There is a generally congested feeling inside the café — when it is crowded there are always a few people standing in the aisle. The stage should look open; a general feeling of looseness should be conveyed in the design of the set and the random wandering of people. The confining factor is their number.

Much of the play consists of several simultaneous conversations in various groups with dialogue either overlapping or interlocking. These sections should flow as a whole, without specific focus; they rise and subside and scenes develop from them.

Everything seems to move in a circle. Within the general large pattern the people who spend their nights at the café have separate goals and separate characters but together they constitute a whole, revolving around some common center. They are the riffraff, the bums, the petty thieves, the scum, the lost, the desperate, the dispossessed, the cool; depending on one's attitude there are a hundred names that could describe them. They live within as rigid a frame, with its own definitions, as any other stratum. Their language, their actions, their reading of morality is individual but strict.

CHARACTERS

A number of "hoods" (A general term that could cover almost everyone in the play, but defines more specifically the petty thieves, bargainers, hagglers, pimps. They will steal anything from anyone and sell anything including themselves to any man or woman with the money, although they could not be described as homosexuals. Their activities in this area are few and not often mentioned.):

BOB

XAVIER

TIG, a male prostitute (hustler).

MARTIN, a heroin addict.

RAKE, a hustler.

DOPEY, a hustler-addict.

ERNESTO, a hustler — Colombian.

Some are junkies as well, as noted, some are hustlers; definitions overlap. Dopey is a heroin addict as well as a sometimes-not-too-good hustler. What they are now is not what they will be a month from now. A number of the men have no special classification; they might have part-time jobs at times; they might do a number of things, but are not involved in any specific activity:

TIM

CARLO, a Colombian.

JOHN, the waiter-grill man.

A number of the girls are lesbians; some have boys' nicknames; they might be prostitutes as well:

TERRY

RUST

JUDY

Other characters include:

FICK, a heroin addict who sometimes provides a background to the rest of the action.

BABE, a heroin addict who sits stony silent at the counter through the first half of the play. (When the set is moved, she walks beside it.)

KAY, the waitress.

FRANNY, an almost transvestite boy — very beautiful, very feminine.

DAVID, much like Franny, not so lovely.

BONNIE, a prostitute.

ANN, a prostitute.

STRANGER, about thirty-five.

FRANK, about fifty-five.

AL, a bum, about fifty.

The production should concentrate on the movement of the whole, slowly focusing on Joe and Darlene:

JOE, a New Yorker, typical middle-class metropolitan background. He is twenty-four, good-looking, of average height and build. He has dark hair. He has a guarded reaction to everything and everyone. He speaks clearly.

DARLENE, an attractive girl, twenty to twenty-three; recently arrived from Chicago; she speaks with a candid, Midwestern voice that sets her apart from the sound of the rest of the play. She is honest, romantic to a fault, and not at all bright. The actress playing Darlene should be aware that she is supposed to be stupid, and not the sweet, girl-next-door, common-sense-saves-the-day type of ingenue.

FOUR BLACK ENTERTAINERS
FOUR CHILDREN

Most of the characters are about twenty-three to thirty years old.

The play covers a week or two just before Halloween. The rock'n'roll song at the beginning and near the end should be accompanied by recording; the round is not accompanied. The pace of the play, except in a few scenes, should be breakneck fast. There is one intermission.

BALM IN GILEAD

ACT ONE

A noise from a crowd begins and reaches a peak as the curtain rises. From the wings come four black entertainers (two from each side) who sing a rock'n'roll song with much clapping, dancing, etc. They are accompanied by a typical clangy, catchy instrumentation. From far out on the apron they sing to the audience — very animated. As the song fades out, and they begin to move (still singing) back of the stage, the noise from the group rises again.

FICK. *(Outside the café, to one of the four singers as the song ends. Fick will talk to anything that moves.)* Hey, fellow, buddy; you got a cigarette? Baby? Hey, fellow — could you — hey, friend? *(They are moving off.)* Screw it. *(To someone else.)* Hey buddy? *(He wanders to the street corner group of Dopey, Ernesto, Joe, and Rake.)*

BOB. *(As one of the singers runs by him he reaches out and grabs his behind. The crowd in the café notices this and laughs. Bob whirls around to them.)* I never seen a singer yet that was goosey! *(Crowd laughs.)*

ERNESTO. Yeah, you watch your mouth! *(He laughs.)*

TIG. *(From the café.)* You just watch that, Terry-boy.

JUDY. All right! Come on. If we're going to get goin' in here, get goin', get that table out of the way, come on; line them up a little. *(A few people straighten the booths into rows.)*

TIG. *(Overlapping.*)* What are you, some kind of housewife, Judy?

*"Overlapping" will indicate that the speech is started during the preceding speech.

11

JUDY. *(To David.)* You're the housewife, aren't you, sweetheart?

DAVID. You're the fishwife, Judy. Fishwife, Fish. Pheew!

FICK. *(On the corner, to Joe.)* Hey, Joe; Joe.

JOE. I'm going in.

DAVID, *(To Judy.)* A better housewife I'd make, sweetheart, than you ever will.

BONNIE. *(To Franny and David.)* You ought to be chased out of the neighborhood. You clog up the air with a lot of fairy dust. Fairy dust.

FRANNY. *(Overlapping.)* Who you calling a name, you truck driver?

FICK. *(To Joe, overlapping.)* Me too, in a minute; you in with Chuckles like they say? I heard you're going to be tying in with him. If I wasn't, hey, such a junk, you think he'd take me?

BONNIE. Who you queers think you are?

DAVID. Who you callin' queer, George!

BOB. Shut up, over there!

JOE. *(To Fick.)* He might, you work on it, okay, Fick?

DOPEY. Get lost, Fick.

FICK. *(To Joe.)* You know why I will? You know why I'll work on that? Because, hey, one thing Chuckles will give you is a good protection, you know? They hear you're tied in with Chuckles they'll leave you alone, baby.

TERRY. *(Over* Fick's speech; she is very drunk.)* All you queens.

JOE. *(Cutting into Fick's speech.)* Okay, Fick, that's enough.

TIG. *(At the counter to pay — someone has bumped him.)* Come on, God.

FRANNY. *(To Terry.)* Why don't you shut up before I beat you over your head with your dildo?

TERRY. You trying to say something?

FICK. *(To Joe.)* I didn't mean anything by it.

JOE. You just talk too much, baby, you know it?

FICK. *(Joking.)* You wouldn't get Chuckles after me, would you? Look at me, man, I'm, hell, I'm weak as a kitten.

FRANNY. *(Over, to Terry.)* Ah, your mother's a whore —

TERRY. You trying to say something?

*"Over" will indicate that the speech is said simultaneously with the preceding speech.

TIG.   (To Frank, counting his change.) What the hell are you talking about —

FRANK.   Why don't you stop coming in here, you don't —

TIG.   What the hell, you're trying to screw —

FRANK.   (Cutting in.) Get on out now.

TIG.   You trying to cheat me outta four bucks, baby, you can't pull —

FRANK.   I never cheat you outta nothing.

TERRY.   (Over, to David and Franny who are watching Tig and Frank.) You queers just sit down, take it easy.

TIG.   I gave you a five, a five, you son of —

FRANK.   You get on out of here.

TIG.   You want to step outside? You want to step out from behind that counter, baby? You watch it, Frank.

JOHN.   (Cutting in.) Come on, Tig, give up, go on out.

FRANK.   Get out of this place.

TIG.   (To John.) Ah, come on, I gave him a five, man, you know what he's trying.

JOHN.   Come on, go on, Tig.

TIG.   (Leaving café for street corner.) You wait, Frank; you'll get yours, buddy.

FRANK.   (After Tig has gone.) Get on out of here, bum!

TIG.   (Yelling back heatedly now.) All right, now, goddamnit I'm out, you just shut your mouth, Frank. You stupid bastard.

FRANK.   You get on, bum!

TIG.   Buddy, you're really gonna get it one day, Frank, and I want to be there to watch it. You're gonna get your head split open, dumb bastard.

FICK.   (This exchange should begin during the exchange above, cued by Frank's "You get on out of here.") You wouldn't do something like that, would you, Joe?

JOE.   Just don't talk so much. What makes you think I even know Chuckles?

FICK.   You're not going to turn him down are you? Something like that?

JOE.   We'll see, won't we?

FICK.   'Cause, man, I wouldn't do that, I know that. Course you're a strong guy, I'm weak as a kitten. That's too much of a hassle for me. I'd take some of Chuckles' protection, man; he — (*Joe pushes him away slightly and walks to the café.*) Yeah, well, nice seeing you, buddy; you come around any time. Any time, we'll talk again, babe, okay? (*Joe enters the café.*)

(*Note that in production, each group, and there are several of them, must maintain a kind of life of its own. The group on the street corner, for instance, usually Rake, Dopey, Tig, and Ernesto, loiter with nothing much to say. Improvised, unheard conversations may be used. Characters may wander along the street and back, improvise private jokes, or stand perfectly still, waiting. The same goes for groups in the café, such as Terry, Rust, and Judy. Their lines should come from scenes developed within the situation. Aside from this, it should be mentioned that everyone in the café [with the exception of Babe and Fick] looks up the moment someone enters the café: a kind of reflex "once-over" to evaluate any new opportunity or threat.*)

TIM. (*At the counter, to Frank.*) Hey, Frank, could I have a hot tea, okay?

FRANK. Shut up. All you hoodlums.

TIM. What the hell did I say? (*To himself.*) I'm kinna drunk.

FRANK. Just shut up that. Hoodlums. This is a decent place; you guys ruin it for everybody!

DAVID. Why the hell you yelling at him; he hasn't done nothing.

TERRY. Shut up, Frank.

TIM. (*Over.*) I didn't say anything.

RUST. (*Running into café.*) Hey, they got Jerry Joe in the can!

BOB. Jerry the fairy?

DAVID. Watch who you're calling names.

RUST. He tried to put the make on a cop.

BOB. They gonna book him?

JOHN. (*To himself.*) Dumb fag.

RUST. Whatta you mean? He tried to put the make on a cop. Hell, yes, they'll book him. He had eight bombinos on him! Man, are they hot for that stuff. (*General crowd reaction.*)

FRANK. Come on, knock it off.

KAY. Fry two, John.

FRANK. I'm going now, Johnnie; you take over.

RUST. I wish I'd seen his face!

FRANK. (*As Dopey tries to enter the café.*) Now keep out. Come on, you know you don't get served, come on get out. Junkies and dopes and whores —

FRANNY.   Who's a whore?

FRANK.   — What kind of a neighborhood is this? I'll go, Johnnie.

BOB.   *(To Frank.)* Swinging.

FRANK.   I'll swing you, right out of here. *(Exits.)*

JOHN.   Come on, now, keep it down.

TIM.   May I have a tea, please?

BONNIE.   *(At a booth, reading a check.)* What the hell is this, fifty cents for one Coke, you think this is the Ritz?

JOHN.   There's a sign right there, fifty cents minimum at booths; if you don t have it, don't sit there.

BONNIE.   Screw it, I'm payin' no fifty cents for one Coke.

KAY.   *(To John.)* Toast with that.

BOB.   Fifty cents you can get a good high.

BONNIE.   Gimme a cheese sandwich; hell, if I'm going to spend a fortune. One goddamned Coke.

KAY.   And a jack.

DAVID.   *(Cutting in — to Bob.)* Come on up to my room, it won't kill you.

BOB.   Knock it off. *(To Ann.)* How much you make tonight, Ann?

ANN.   Huh?

DAVID.   *(Joking more than anything.)* Come on up with me, it won't kill you.

BOB.   How much scratch? Jack? Tonight?

ANN.   None of your damn business. Ask Sammy, you want to know.

TIG.   *(Has wandered back in; he is standing near Ann.)* You still keepin' that bum? What's he do with all that dough?

ANN.   He banks it. Or at least he'd better be banking it.

BOB.   Yeah, he banks it with Cameron or Chuckles.

ANN.   He don't truck with that junk. He'd better not; I'd crack him over the head.

TIG.   Feed him bennies you'll keep him limp — he won't go messing around.

KAY.   *(To Bonnie.)* Whatta you want on the cheese?

ANN.   I don't need him limp; limp for five minutes he can limp out in the ever-loving street.

15

BONNIE. I don't care — Christ.

BOB. Who's name does he bank it in?

TIG. Come on, how much you clear last night?

ANN. Clear? It's all clear; what do you think I do make out an income-tax report?

DAVID. *(To Bob.)* You comin' up?

BONNIE. Hey, Kay, make that a cheeseburger.

JOE. *(To Ann.)* He keeps at it — I like his drive.

ANN. I like sex drive.

KAY. Make up your mind!

JOE. That's all you ever think about. I'm working now, I tell you.

ANN. You think I don't work? I'll show you my bunions.

JOHN. *(To Terry.)* Whatta you want for a quarter? (*Suddenly lights dim into full blink for a second only. Dim on all of café; spot on Joe. Held for a second only, with no reaction anywhere else.*)

KAY. Onions on that?

BOB. *(To Ann.)* I got something you could use.

KAY. You want onions on that?

DAVID. Well, are you?

BOB. No, I'm not coming up! Look, I don't dig boys; fags. Understand? Not unless you got a roll on you.

DAVID. Don't knock it till you've tried it.

BOB. I happen to like tits. You got tits? *(General laughter.)*

BONNIE. And another Coke. Put some ice in it this time, okay?

ANN. Come on up, Joe. I won't bite you. Sammy's out.

JOE. I told you I'm a working boy, now.

ANN. Yeah, I'll bet. You pushing your box? Hustling it down to Forty-second?

JOE. Who, me? Not on your life.

KAY. *(Calling to John.)* All the way.

BONNIE. *(To Kay.)* Grilled onions, why not.

JOHN *(To David who is leaving.)* You pay?

ANN. You are; I'll bet.

DAVID. Yes, I paid; I paid half an hour ago.

BOB. You get tits, you come back and let me know.

DAVID. You go to hell. Who needs you? (*David leaves café as Martin enters, almost bumping into him.*) Watch out, for Christ's sake. (*Exits. Martin spots Joe from across the café.*)

16

ANN. Come on up, Joe.

MARTIN. Joe, hey!

ANN. Hey, John; give me another coffee. You're getting worse than Frank.

JOHN. Watch your language.

ANN. What'd I say?

MARTIN. Hey, Joe, you got any?

JOHN. You said Frank. *(Ann laughs.)*

JOE. Any what?

MARTIN. You know. Come on.

TIG. *(Ordering.)* Plain Pepsi.

JOE. What you want with me? I got nothing you want.

ANN. *(To Joe.)* You got something I want.

TIG. No ice.

MARTIN. Joe, no kiddin', I gotta. Man, you don't know! Don't play games with me, baby.

JOE. I'm not playing games, Martin. *(The quartette have entered café and are standing in back. They harmonize in an off-key improvisation a rock'n'roll song, with someone using a table for a drum.)*

BOB. Hey, Tig.

MARTIN. Just one, Joe. I gotta, man. You don't know.

TIG. *(To Bob.)* Yeah, what's in it for me, huh?

JOHN. *(To Ann.)* You wanted coffee. Cream?

TIM. I think I'm gonna be sick.

JUDY. *(To Tim.)* You okay?

MARTIN. Come on, baby.

JOE. Go where you usually go.

JUDY. You want a tomato juice or something?

TIM. God, no.

JOHN. Cream, Ann?

TIM. Okay.

ANN. Black.

JOE. Go where you usually go.

TIM. No I don't, either.

ANN. You got the lousiest service.

MARTIN. I go to Jerry Joe.

BOB. *(Overhears, turns around, then back.)* Jerry the fairy?

MARTIN. Yeah, well, Jerry the fairy's in the can. In the box, man. Come on, Joe. You got any? I heard you could.

JOE.   You go to Jerry Joe? That's a sad turn of events.

TIM.   I'm all right.

MARTIN.   Don't play with me, baby. What's the matter with you guys, you think as soon as you get a pinch to push you can play games and play big shot with everyone.

JOE.   I'm not playing games, Martin. I'm your friend. I don't follow what you're talking about is all. You're not making sense.

MARTIN.   Come on, Jerry Joe's in the can. *(Phone rings — John goes to answer.)*

JOE.   Look Martin. If I was just starting out — I couldn't take on the whole neighborhood, now, could I?

MARTIN.   Why not, man; corner the market.

JOHN.   *(On the phone.)* What?

JOE.   Yeah, and get cornered.

FRANNY.   *(To Tig.)* Have you seen Lilly?

JOHN.   *(Holding the phone.)* Anybody here named Carol?

FRANNY.   If that's my husband, tell him I dropped dead. *(Exits.)*

ANN.   If that's Sammy, tell him I'm turning a trick. *(All laugh.)* Under the table. *(Laughs.)*

BONNIE.   You could do it too.

ANN.   If anybody could, honey. *(John hangs up the phone.)*

TIM.   Could I have another tea, John.

JOHN.   Sure. *(Tig gets up to leave.)*

JOE.   Why don't you go somewhere else, come on.

MARTIN.   'Cause I come to you. What the hell's wrong? Come on, buddy.

TIG.   *(Yelling to John.)* Hey, what time you get off?

JOHN.   Seven in the morning.

TIG.   Whatta you work, seven to seven?

JOHN.   Yeah. Swingin' hours, huh?

TIG.   Christ! *(Leaves café for street corner.)*

MARTIN.   What's wrong, huh? I come to you.

ERNESTO.   *(Enters the café from the street corner.)* Coffee. Lottsa cream. No, black. Black. And a chocolate cupcake. How much is a cake?

JOHN.   Twenty-five. Big one's thirty.

ERNESTO.   Just the coffee's okay. Black. Black.

ANN.   Black.

JOHN.   Black.

JOE.   Look! *(Fick enters over Joe's line and begins his long wandering dialogue.)* Look! Martin, baby. *(Sudden dim again. Spot on Joe and Martin. Everyone holds their positions. Stop-motion. Fick's dialogue and movement continue over the pause as though nothing else were happening.)* Look.... You come back about ten o'clock. And I'll see. Okay? *(Spot dims on Joe and Martin and then natural lighting resumes.)*

JOHN.   *(Fakes a blow to Ernesto's side.)* Come on, I'll show you. Take that. Pow!

ERNESTO.   *(Fake reaction. Sudden violence here, though it is only a kind of horsing around.)* Gad, in the liver — I'll get you for that one....

TIG.   *(On the corner. Slaps someone on the back.)* You're a pal.

ERNESTO.   *(To John.)* You're a pal! *(Bob leaves café for street corner.)*

ANN.   *(Very rapid exchange here. To Ernesto.)* You're a pal.

MARTIN.   You're a pal, Joe! You're great! *(Hesitantly.)* You're sure? *(Starts to go.)* Sure?

JOE.   Ten o'clock. I'll see you. Don't go talking to anyone, okay?

MARTIN.   You know me, I'm your friend.

JOHN.   *(To Martin.)* Did you pay?

MARTIN.   You don't know how cheap you make a fellow look. Asking did he pay. You make people look cheap talking like that. You make people feel cheap talking like that. *(Exits.)*

FICK.   *(This dialogue begins in the background of the scene above at Joe's first "Look!" Very softly.)* Man, it's getting cold out there, isn't it? Hey, John, fix me up with a coffee, could you? Warm up a little bit, you know what I mean? That's no good, walking around out there dressed like I am in this weather, I mean it isn't cold yet, but it's getting there and I'm not going to be dressed any warmer in another month when it comes. Kid like me. That's no good for you — you know, with alcohol you're not so bad because it's in your bloodstream, you know, but with horse like I take you got to watch out 'cause you don't notice the cold and the first thing you know you're sick as a bitch, man, and about all I need is to go into a hospital or something like that and let them start looking me over, you know? That's about like all I need, man. What is it, about

19

October? About the middle of October, huh? Damn it'll be getting really cold before long. You know what I mean?

BOB.   Hey, Tig, I got something you'd like I bet. Hey Dopey.

TIG.   What?

RUST.   *(To Kay.)* Miss, could I have a soup?

ANN.   *(To Joe.)* What are you into now?

TERRY.   *(To Kay.)* Two, okay? What is it?

DOPEY.   Yeah, what?

BOB.   I'll bet.

KAY.   *(To Terry.)* Bean — lima.

JOE.   What do you mean?

ANN.   What are you into now?

RUST.   Christ. Well, okay.

JOE.   Come on, keep it down.

ANN.   *(Standing up.)* Well, I gotta go, if you aren't coming up.
You just watch yourself, Joey buddy. *(She pays her bill.)*

KAY.   Two soup, Johnnie.

JOE.   Damnit, don't worry about me. I know what I'm doing.

FRANNY.   *(Reenters the café.)* Has anybody seen Red tonight?
(Ann exits.)

JOE.   *(To Franny, making up for being irritated by Ann.)* Not since
last night, baby.

FRANNY.   *(Flat.)* Jerry Joe's in the can. Had about a dozen
bombinos on him.

JOE.   *(To Franny, irritated suddenly.)* Go get laid, why don't you?

DOPEY.   *(On the corner; to Rake.)* I tell you I kicked it.

FRANNY.   *(To Joe over.)* Who's tickling your ass? Be like that, I
don't need you. You're working for Chuckles now?

JOE.   Mind your own, sweetheart; you live longer.

RAKE.   Sure.

JUDY.   *(To Terry.)* I'll be back. *(She goes to Tim.)*

DOPEY.   No, I did. Yes, I did.

RAKE.   Hell you did.

DOPEY.   I will, you wait.

TIM.   I'm sick. I knew I was.

KAY.   *(With soup, to Rust and Terry.)* It's hot.

JUDY.   You okay?

FRANNY.   Chuckles can kiss it, honey; my second husband was a pusher. I don't owe him nothing; he's not my type.

JOE. *(Getting up.)* Why don't....

TERRY. *(From the back of the café, regarding Judy.)* Now she thinks she's some kind of wet nurse.

RUST. *(To Terry.)* One's just like the other. *(Bob and Tig enter café from corner. Al enters café from offstage.)*

JUDY. Hey, Rake. Over here. *(Rake leaves the corner, enters the café, looks around.)*

JOHN. *(To Rake.)* Come on, come on, Rake. We can't serve you. Run out on checks — go on, back out in the street, Rake. You know that.

RAKE. *(To John.)* Screw you. *(Exits to corner.)*

CARLO. *(Enters. To Tim.)* Hello.

TIM. *(Sick.)* Not now, Carlo.

CARLO. *Ernesto, ¿cómo está?*

AL. Give me a coffee, okay? Noisy, ain't it?

KAY. Coffee, okay.

TIM. *(Gets up, Judy follows him, trying to take him home.)* Damn, I think I'm sick. None of you are worth a good —

ERNESTO. Carlo.

JUDY. Come on you're drunk as a judge. Come on, let's get you home or somewhere, okay?

ERNESTO. *(To Carlo.)* ¿Qué pasa, Chico?

TIM. Carlo can hardly speak English even. *(To Judy.)* Take your hands. Not worth a damn. *(Staggers forward.)* Take your — dike, you go with girls. Mess around with your own kind.

TERRY. *(Over.)* I don't care where she sleeps or who she sleeps with!

JUDY. Come on.

TIM. Take your hands off me, you go with girls. You're a whatsit. *(Aside to the audience.)* She's a whatsit, without a gizmo.

JUDY. Come on, you're drunk.

TIM. At least I'm drunk on drunk, not on junk like everyone....

JUDY. Come on, Tim, you're drunk. You're sick, Timmy.

TIM. I'm *sick? (To audience.)* *I'm* sick? She's a thingamabob!

JUDY. Come on, go on home, Tim.

TIM. *(To audience.)* Listen! *(Aside, to himself.)* Oh, damn; I'll bet I've been drinking again. *(To audience.)* Now you listen! Damnit, this is important! *(Judy turns him around and they move toward the door. Over his shoulder to the audience.)* Now you watch this. Here.

FICK.   Terry, you got a cigarette, huh?

AL.   *(To Tig.)* She's gonna take him!

TERRY.   *(To Fick.)* Come on, get lost.

KAY.   *(To Judy.)* What'd you have?

JUDY.   I'll be back! *(Judy and Tim exit as Darlene enters.)*

TERRY.   She can sleep in the damn hall for all I care!

RUST.   *(To Terry.)* I don't get it.

AL.   It happens every time. Did you see that?

BOB.   *(Looks up as Darlene enters the café.)* Well, dig that. *(Darlene sits at counter, John comes to wait on her.)*

AL.   You get hurt, see? Every time. And then finally you learn not to pay any attention to anything.

TIG.   Yeah, I know. Well, don't let it bother you.

BOB.   *(To Darlene.)* Can I buy you a cup coffee? Can I just buy you maybe? Look, I got thirty cents somewhere.

AL.   And then you just don't let anything bother you at all.

DARLENE.   *(To John.)* Coffee, please.

AL.   And you still get hurt.

JOHN.   *(To Darlene.)* Right.

KAY.   *(Yelling to John from back.)* Draw one!

BOB.   You belong here? You new?

KAY.   *(Yelling to John.)* Two!

TIG.   *(Interested in Darlene now.)* She's not the talkative type.

DARLENE.   *(Quietly slips off the stool. To John.)* Never mind. *(She turns to go but there is a crowd at the door. Bob stands in front of her.)*

TIG.   Well, don't run off, sweetheart.

FICK.   *(From the back.)* It's cold — it gets cold.

DARLENE.   Come on.

BOB.   I'm sorry if I'm in your way, but I can't move. Look.

DARLENE.   Come on, I'm leaving.

TERRY.   She can sleep in the alley for all I care!

TIG.   Oh, am I in your way?

DARLENE.   Oh, screw it. Go away. *(Turns to the counter and sits again.)*

JOHN.   *(To Darlene.)* You order coffee?

TIG.   You're new. You know anyone around here?

BOB.   Well, be a little sociable anyway. *(Franny in exiting bumps against Bob, Bob against Darlene.)* Hey, I'm sorry. *(Turns around, to Franny.)* Watch where you're going!

FRANNY.   Oh, suck it; if you were sober maybe you could stand up. *(Exits.)*

TIG.   What are you, mad at the world?

RUST.   And she better *stay* gone.

BOB.   *(To Tig.)* Screw it, forget her. Let's go. *(Dopey enters café, takes a seat.)*

JOHN.   Come on, Dopey, you're going to fall asleep.

TIG.   Don't bother to speak. *(Goes to the back of café.)*

BOB.   Screw it.

DOPEY.   What do you mean, I'm awake. Look! I want a cup of coffee.

JOHN.   I know, but I'll give it to you and you'll be asleep on the damn table. You do it every time, Dopey. *(John turns to get him coffee.)*

KAY.   *(To Bob who has stopped in the doorway.)* Come on, you're holdin' the door open!

TERRY.   *(Much louder.)* I don't give a good goddamn if she sleeps with Margaret Truman! *(Bob exits.)*

DOPEY.   *(To prove he's awake.)* Kay? Could you hand me the cream, please? *(At the back of the café Terry falls against a booth. Much commotion. She has spilled coffee on Bonnie. They sit her down again.)*

RUST, BONNIE, TERRY.   *(Variously.)*

    Come on.

    God, look at that all over me!

    Where the hell.

    For Christ's sake, where the hell are you going?

    Watch it, fellow.

    Sit down, take it easy.

    All over me. Goddamn.

    Do you have a rag?

    Miss? Now just take it easy.

    Why don't you sober up?

(Lights dim for only a second, during the above exchange, with a spot on Darlene.)

AL.   *(To John.)* They every one of them steal. They all steal, you know?

TIG.   *(To Ernesto.)* Spices and things, you know. *(Ann reenters.)*

JOHN.   Yeah. Well. *(Darlene and Joe exchange several glances.)*

AL.   Every girl you see; they all steal. You take them up to your room and they'll steal something every time. You fall asleep and they'll sneak out and steal something.

TERRY.   *(Over, from the back.)* I'm sorry. I'm sorry. I am. *(Dopey is falling asleep on the table.)*

AL.   And then they tell you they left the door open.

JOHN.   I know. No, I don't, but I know.

AL.   They all steal. *(Momentary lull. The quartette begins a soft blues from the back.)*

JOHN.   When it gets quiet in here you almost think something's gonna happen.

KAY.   Quiet all of a sudden, ain't it?

ANN.   *(To John.)* You want somebody should scream or something?

JOHN.   Oh, go back out on the street!

ANN.   It's dirty out there. I think I'm going to write to the Department of Sanitation. I made sixty tonight.

JOHN.   Sixty scores or sixty bills?

ANN.   Four scores — ha! — and thirty-eight cents. I always end up with odd change; never can figure out where the hell it came from.

JOHN.   You're so rich, so buy me a drink, teacher.

ANN.   Sammy would slug me, I spend his money on you.

TERRY.   She can just kiss it.

JOHN.   Why do you keep him anyway?

ANN.   God, you'd better go back to school.

RUST.   Miss, could we have another coffee? Two more. *(Darlene moves her cup now to the seat by Joe. Takes the seat next to him.)*

DARLENE.   Do you mind?

JOE.   How should I mind?

DARLENE.   Well, look, if you're thinking or waiting for someone....

JOE.   No, I'm not waiting for someone.

DARLENE.   I saw you looking at the clock.

JOE.   I'm waiting for ten o'clock. (*He drinks. She takes a cigarette out, he lights hers and his own.*)

DARLENE.   Thanks.

TIG.   (*To Ernesto.*) You know in Egypt they had salves and things that could cure anything.

DARLENE.   That's better than those other two creeps were acting. Did you see them?

JOE.   They're just high. They're okay usually.

TIG.   Cancer even! It says so.

ERNESTO.   Show me where, you can't.

TIG.   It does.

DARLENE.   Why are you waiting for ten o'clock?

TIG.   Hey, John; you ever read the Bible?

JOE.   I'm meeting someone.

JOHN.   What?

TIG.   The Bible, stupid.

JOE.   Like a business deal. A transaction.

JOHN.   Sure. When I was about twelve.

ERNESTO.   Yeah?

JOHN.   I didn't understand it.

TIG.   Hell, you wouldn't anyway. You know they had embalming fluid back then?

AL.   What'd they do, drink it?

ERNESTO.   Show me where.

TIG.   Go away.

DARLENE.   What were they high on?

JOE.   Huh? How should I know? (*Ernesto pays check and exits to corner.*)

DARLENE.   On dope, or just drinking?

JOE.   You don't get high on ginger. Bombinos, deedees; you don't scream it out — you know, you don't yell it out like that.

DARLENE.   Do you like that?

JOE.   Are you kidding?

DARLENE.   Me either — eye-ther.

JOE.   Not on your life. Once is enough.

DARLENE.   Oh. What was it like?

JOE.   Are you kidding? Like getting sick as a bitch. Depends on what you're taking though. New, are you?

25

DARLENE. Well, have you seen me before?

JOE. No.

DARLENE. Are you sure?

JOE. Yeah.

DARLENE. How do you know?

JOE. I'd know.

DARLENE. *(Complimented.)* Thanks.

JOE. I remember faces. You see me standing around, you'd think I was just as stupid as the next guy, but I look — and I watch people, you know? And I study them when they don't know. You learn a lot. Where you from?

DARLENE. I'm from Chicago.

TIG. *(Comes from the booth to John at the cash register.)* Could I have change for cigarettes?

DARLENE. *(Pausing.)* My sister used to come around here, though. She's living off somewhere right now.

JOE. Who's your sister?

DARLENE. Oh, you wouldn't know her. It must have been four years ago. She used to write me.

TIG. *(Hits the machine.)* This damn thing!

DARLENE. Sometimes.

JOE. What'd she do?

DARLENE. Oh, I don't know. *(Affected.)* We used to exchange letters. She'd write and I'd think, God — New York! *(Pause.)* She was ... like her. *(Nods to Ann.)* Of course, she was very pretty, you know.

JOE. Ann? A hooker. She sold it?

DARLENE. Well, you needn't be high and mighty about it.

JOE. Who is?

DARLENE. She used to make — sometimes a hundred dollars a night ... twice that sometimes.

JOE. So does Ann, but she loves it. *(Yelling out.)* Don't you, Ann?

ANN. Don't I what?

JOE. Just say yes.

ANN. No. Hell, no; it's a lie if he's saying it. *(Turns away.)*

JOE. She goes for free as much as she charges.

DARLENE. She didn't come here for that, of course. She came here to do something else. I forget what; you know. But you look

26

and you don't get anything and you — resort, you know? To something else.

RUST. *(To Terry.)* I wouldn't worry about it.

JOE. Naw, Ann didn't either. Ann's a schoolteacher. Was going to be; came here to do something like that. When she got here they tell her she can work part-time or something.

TERRY. It doesn't affect me.

JOE. She told 'em to kiss it. She got a raw deal.

DARLENE. Yeah. You know what I'd make as a waitress? Maybe sixty dollars a week. Less maybe. Tips included.

JOE. You been here long?

DARLENE. A month.

JOE. Month? You must have saved up.

DARLENE. Are you kidding? I came here with about seven dollars.

JOE. You get a room around here yet?

DARLENE. I'm across the street, in the Towers. And probably I'll get....

JOE. And one upstairs? Everybody does.

DARLENE. My sister had a room; this same place. I didn't ask you what your ten-o'clock business deal was.

JOE. Yeah, you did.

DARLENE. Well, I didn't care. *(Pause.)* It's a filthy place upstairs. Have you seen it up there? I looked around this afternoon already. I've never seen cockroaches like that. I mean they should get a bravery medal or something. They play games on the floor right in front of you. They don't even run from you. *(Dopey has awakened. He looks at his coffee and gets up to leave.)*

KAY. *(To Dopey.)* Hey, you pay?

DOPEY. I don't have anything.

KAY. Coffee.

DOPEY. I didn't even touch it. I gotta get outside. *(He leaves café for corner.)*

JOE. You know I might be able to help you get a room. Save you some dough, maybe. After the first week or two they'll get on to you and kick you out. They got fellas that hang around to spot girls who take people up. You'll have to get one of the boys around to rent a room in his name and then he'll rent it to you. See? They

27

don't really care, just so long as they look legal. Most of the guys, though, would make you pay through the nose.

DARLENE.   Why? I mean why should I get a room from someone else? *(Judy enters and goes to cash register.)*

JOE.   It's just the way you have to do it. All these guys in here — a lot of them — they rent a room out for about eight bucks a night. That's not much when you're making a hundred.

KAY.   *(To Judy.)* You owe for a burger and a Coke.

JUDY.   I'll get it.

DARLENE.   It sounds like a lot to me. Eight dollars a day? A room's only twelve a week. No girl's gonna do that.

JOE.   They got nothing better to do with their money. Most of the girls keep a fellow anyway. Give most of their money to some guy. Then he treats them like shit. Don't ask me. Over half of them. So they can be seen with someone steady, you know.

JUDY.   *(Regarding Rust and Terry in the back booth.)* Well, isn't that cozy?

DARLENE.   I wouldn't believe it. *(Joe shrugs.)* I mean I believe it, but how can they ever get any money saved up or anything? If they're giving it away? It's pretty sick, isn't it? Everybody living off everybody like that?

JOE.   You won't get away from that, I don't care where you go. You'll either make a mint of money or go broke. But like I said, most guys would charge eight bucks. I could probably get you a room for maybe only four or five.

DARLENE.   I don t think so.

JUDY.   *(To Kay.)* How much do I owe you?

JOE.   You'll either go broke or make a pile.

KAY.   Ninety-five and that guy's two teas.

DARLENE.   I made two hundred dollars one night. That's what I've been living off of. One guy; man, one night.

JUDY.   Just me; he can come back and pay.

JOE.   Don't expect it every time. *(Rust comes up to the counter.)*

DARLENE.   And I didn't have to do anything.

RUST.   Give me a glass of water, Kay.

JOE.   Much.

KAY.   Just hold it a minute!

DARLENE.   Nothing. He felt sorry for me or something. He was

28

a customer — in this café? And the boss fired me. I was right out on the floor and got fired on the spot. And this guy came over to me on the floor and said, let's go have a steak or something to eat, you don't want to work here anyway. Let's go have a steak. He was my first customer at the café. I walked right off the floor and we went to his room and he gave me two hundred dollars.

RUST.   Could I have a glass of water?

JOE.   What, did you roll him?

JUDY.   *(To Rust.)* First things first, honey!

DARLENE.   No! I told you. He gave it to me. He felt sorry for me or something. *(Dopey has been standing on the corner, talking to Rake. He turns to the audience, walks a little away from the others. The action continues in the café behind him during this speech.)*

DOPEY.   What he's saying — about renting rooms and all — see — well, there's no reason for it but when a girl — or around here anyway most of the girls have a guy that — kinna looks after them. After all, it's a rough neighborhood; but that's not the only way he looks after them, if you follow my meaning. And the girl sorta keeps him. The guys that are lucky. He lives up in the room — sleeps in the day and the girl uses the room at night. Maybe you think they're being exploited — the girls, I mean, because they don't get ahead. Every dime goes to the john — that's the fellow. And he eventually pulls out — runs off with it — after he's stashed it in a savings account somewhere. But these girls aren't getting so much exploited because they need these guys. No one's forcing them. One leaves, then right after they get over it they're out looking for someone else. Only someone *better.* You know? Like Ann is probably half expecting her john — this guy's name's Sam, or Sammy: she's half expecting him to leave. He's been around seven or eight months; that's about par for Ann. *(Pause.)* Well, it's because they want someone around and because after all balling with old men all the time can get to be a drag — of course not all of their scores are old men. They get just as many good-looking guys; young fellows; high school kids and like that, they pay. Well, maybe you don't like to hear that but they do. So it's not that they get sick of the old men all the time. But these guys that they ball, they aren't — around. You know? They aren't *around.* They want probably to know someone probably. See they're — well. And they don't get new things! I mean these girls don't go out and get themselves dresses and jewelry and things. I mean they get things, but not for themselves, see; for the guy who's with them. New clothes and rings and stuff — all kinds of crap and well because it's no kind of a lark crawling in and out of bed all night and in the morning they maybe want someone who won't leave, see. Won't get up and take off. *(Very quick.)* And then they buy these guys things so the guys around can see how they keep their johns in luxury, you know. *(Pause.)* It's natural as anything. They want someone familiar. You know — to know somebody's touch or their manner or like the texture of his skin. Even if the guy's still asleep in the morning. You can picture it. And this usually keeps them from getting much else. That's what he's trying to tell her only she'll know after a while anyway because it's just a natural thing. So she'll find it out anyway but not till she's there herself.

JUDY.   *(To Kay.)* Don't forget the little bitch's glass of water?

RUST.   *(To Judy.)* Who're you talking to?

JUDY.   She's gotta wash out a bad taste in her mouth.

RUST.   You talking to me, you talk to me.

JUDY.   You just take it for what it's worth.

RUST.   You got something to say, say it.

FICK.   You got a light, Ann?

JUDY.   Go on back to the peach in the corner.

JOHN.   *(To Rust.)* Sit back down, I'll bring it to you.

RUST.   *(Returning to her seat.)* Tell her to shut her filthy mouth.

JUDY.   You want to know what a filthy mouth is?

JOHN.   Come on....

JUDY.   I'll rub your face in the sewer you try to....

JOHN.   Come on, sit down or get out now.

JUDY.   *(Sitting immediately.)* Give me a coffee! *(Rust sits down at the booth. Dopey walks away from the audience and then comes back, a new thought. A bit irritated.)*

DOPEY.   You know, though, what — I was thinking what she said; before that, about the cockroaches and all upstairs and she's right, it's a crawling bughouse up there; what really gripes me, she mentioned all the roaches playing like games on the floor up there. A roach's *attitude* just gripes the hell out of me. But what burns me, I've been reading up, not recently, but I saw it somewhere where not only was the roach — that same, exact, goddamn roach that we know — not only were they around about two million years before man, you know, before we came along: Anthropologists or whatever, geologists over in Egypt or somewhere, looking for the first city, they dug down through a city, and straight on down through another, you know, they're piled up like a sandwich or in layers like a seven-layer cake. And they cut down, down through one century to the one before it and the one before that, and every one they found more goddamned cockroaches than anything, and they got before man ever existed and like in the basement of the whole works, there those damn bugs still were, so they've been around, like I said for about a million years before we came along. But not only that! They've made tests, and they found out that a roach can stand — if there was going to be a big atom explosion, they can stand something like *fourteen times* as much radio-whatever-it-is, you-know-activity as we can. So after every man, woman, and child is wiped out and gone, like you imagine, those same goddamn cockroaches will be still crawling around happy as you please over the ruins of everything. Now the picture of that really gripes my ass. *(He wanders into the café.)*

JOE. *(Reaches into his pocket.)* Did you ever see one of these?

DARLENE. What? What is it, an hourglass?

JOE. Yeah, that lasts about three hours. That's a bombino. That's what Bob had. You asked how he got high.

DARLENE. I don't want it!

JOE. I'm not about to give it to you. It's worth money.

DOPEY. Coffee.

DARLENE. How's it work?

JOHN. Aw, come on, Dopey. You'll just go asleep.

JOE. It works wonders. See?

DOPEY. Whatta you mean? *(John ignores him this time.)*

JOE. That's one jolt in each side. And you break it open, see, and take a tube, a needle and a —

DARLENE. A needle? Oh, God. I thought that's what —*(Joe makes a motion injecting it into his arm.)* That's terrible! That just makes my knees weak.

JOE. I better not let anyone see me doing that; they'll think I'm really taking it. *(Darlene laughs.)* That's the easy way. I just got one of these. Mostly it's heroin, and that and some of the others you heat up in a spoon with a match.

DARLENE.   I don't want to hear it.

JOE.   It's a lotta trouble.

DARLENE.   And they pay for it?

JOE.   Sure. They love it. You gotta sorta coax them along; play with them. They have to get it and they expect it to be tough to get.

BONNIE.   *(At counter.)* That's highway robbery.

DARLENE.   They have to have it. That sounds awful.

JOHN.   *(To Bonnie.)* Everybody makes a living.

JOE.   That's the idea. It doesn't happen overnight or anything.

BONNIE.   I'm not complaining. *(Xavier enters.)*

DARLENE.   How much does it cost you?

JUDY.   *(To Bonnie.)* You get sick of it back there?

JOE.   Usually about four. I can make maybe thirty bucks on a carton. Sometimes more. The goofballs are worth about twice as much profit. But they're the devil. They're wild. You never know what the hell they're going to do to someone.

JUDY.   What are they saying?

XAVIER.   Hey, Joe!

BONNIE.   I'm not in it; whatever you're thinking.

JOE.   Hi, there, buddy.

JUDY.   Well then, just stay out of it then.

XAVIER.   You goin' down to Forty-second later?

JOE.   Naw, not tonight. I thought I'd turn in.

XAVIER.   Nothing's doing down there anyway.

JOE.   Stick around here. Where you been the last two days, man?

XAVIER.   Around. Sleeping around.

JOE.   You still talking about going off? Your old man going to send you some dough?

XAVIER.   I don't know. I don't think so, though. I think maybe I'd like to go to Paris, it's better there. People come back from there they say it's wonderful. Beautiful girls.

JOE.   So what's wrong with the girls here?

XAVIER.   *(Laughing.)* Maybe they all know me.

JOE.   Maybe. Your friends think Paris is great, huh?

XAVIER.   If I go and it's wonderful as that, I'd stay. *(Babe coughs.*

Looks up dreamily and around. Sinks back down. Xavier looks around to her and back.) Maybe girls here aren't so beautiful. *(Laughs.)*

JOE.   Oh, don't look at Babe. Nobody's like her, man.

DARLENE.   What's wrong with her?

XAVIER.   She's very bad off.

DARLENE.   I've been looking at her.

JOE.   You're telling me she's bad off.

XAVIER.   She's — you know — that's no good. She can't go a few hours, I bet. She has to have another. She's on her way right out of it. When they get that bad. On her way off.

DARLENE.   She's on her way off that stool, anyway.

XAVIER.   No, no. A junkie never falls off a stool. They lean out and lean out and they get just to the point and they're way out and their seat is way over there and they start slipping off the stool, and they start shifting back, moving back the other way. A drunk will go right off — *pow* — like that — one jerk and he's on the floor. But a junkie never falls off. You see if I'm wrong.

DARLENE.   I didn't know that.

XAVIER.   You see if I'm wrong. Look, I'll see you.

JOE.   No, come on; stick around.

XAVIER.   I'll be back in a few minutes. *(Exits.)*

JOE.   He runs around all the time. He says he'll see you soon and you don't meet him for a month. He's a nice guy. *Xavier. (He gives it a Spanish pronunciation.)*

DARLENE.   What?

JOE.   They call him *Xavier*. He's Colombian. His old man owns a bunch of hardware stores down there. He's up here though — and the old man won't give him a cent.

DARLENE.   I think he'd be better off back there, then. Is he working?

JOE.   Huh? I don't know what he does. He's going to Paris or somewhere next summer.

DARLENE.   Huh. What was his name?

JOE.   *(In English.)* Xavier.

DARLENE.   No, the other one.

JOE.   *Xavier.* The same thing in Spanish. Like Joe and *José*, you know?

DARLENE.   Yeah. Oh.

JOE.   *(Holding the bombino out in his closed hand.)* You want this?

DARLENE.   Me? No, no. I don't want that.

JOE.   Not to take, I thought maybe you'd want it for a gift to remember me.

DARLENE.   I don't think so. Thanks. What if I got caught with it or something. Then where would I be?

JOE.   It wouldn't be no worse than getting caught taking some guy up to your room. Same thing. Trouble either way you look.

ERNESTO.   *(From the corner.)* Hey, Joe. Have you seen Bob? *(Ernesto and Rake enter the café.)*

RAKE.   Yeah, you seen him?

JOE.   *(Gets up.)* Yeah, he went up to around Eightieth Street.

RAKE.   What time?

JOE.   *(Turns.)* What time, Darlene? The fellow in the orange jacket?

DARLENE.   Oh, just a few minutes ago.

ANN.   I better be going back out into the dirty street.

JOHN.   Yeah, make a little dough.

DARLENE.   About fifteen minutes or so ago, I'd imagine.

ANN.   Dough's ass; I'm tired.

BONNIE.   Back trouble, honey? I know what you mean. You seen King?

ANN.   You seen Sam?

JOHN.   *(To Ernesto and Rake.)* You gonna order?

BONNIE.   Not tonight I haven't.

ANN.   Neither have I, the bastard.

ERNESTO.   Ain't I a steady paying customer?

JOHN.   Are you?

ERNESTO.   I am when I got the dough. You find me a john, I'll buy something. Okay? *(To Joe.)* A few minutes ago? I'll see you around. How late you gonna be here?

JOE.   Ten, eleven. I'm leaving early.

JOHN.   Come on, Rake; you guys. You're blocking the door.

ERNESTO.   I'll see you around. *(To Darlene.)* So long.

RAKE.   See you. *(They drift back to the corner. Dopey gets up, tired of waiting for service and wanders out.)*

DOPEY.   Shit. Try to get served here.

DARLENE.   You saw my name on my purse.

JOE.   Yeah.

DARLENE.   You said it like we'd been introduced and known each other for years.

JUDY.   *(At far end of counter, as Rust leaves the booth again.)* You really cozy back there, are you?

RUST.   What?

JOE.   A queer named Jerry Joe got pinched last night. He used to pick up some scores around here. You know? And they caught him with a dozen bombinos on him.

JUDY.   You cozy back there?

RUST.   Whatta you mean?

JUDY.   Whatta you mean, whatta I mean? I got eyes.

DARLENE.   The pills?

RUST.   Well, whatta you see?

JUDY.   I got eyes, goddamnit. I can see.

JOE.   The other. The pills would have been worse.

RUST.   Why don't you go back there, you're so worried.

DARLENE.   You better watch yourself then.

JUDY.   Go back there! I've had about enough of you.

JOE.   They didn't pick him up for that. That's what I was saying. You're telling *me* I'm in a dangerous business.

RUST.   Nothing's happening you can't see.

JOE.   They picked him up because the stupid fairy tried to pick up a cop. That could happen just as easy to you, you don't play it careful.

JUDY.   You sawed-off little bitch, you moving in? You moving into our pad?

DARLENE.   I guess you take your chances.

RUST.   It'd serve you right if I did.

JUDY.   I've had about enough of you.

RUST.   Go back to your sick friend.

JOE.   It turned out good for me. One of his guys — Martin — came to me already. I'll probably get a few more. He had his finger in everything, Jerry Joe.

JUDY.   Get your hot little ass out of here, now.

JOE.   Push a little; sell a little. Man, I bet he looked funny when that cop flashed his badge. Serves him right for being so stupid.

TERRY.   *(Standing up, very drunk.)* Just can it now, Judy. Nothing's happening.

FICK. *(To John.)* Could I have a coffee? I think. And a bowl of soup? It's getting cold out, huh?

RUST. I'm gonna get this bitch out of my hair.

JOHN. *(To Rust and Judy.)* Watch it now. *(Phone rings. John goes to it, answers it.)*

RUST. *(Flares up now.)* You're not gonna get nothing.

JUDY. I'm gonna teach you to break everyone up.

RUST. You're gonna get your ass kicked is what you're gonna get!

JUDY. You little bitch, you can just get the — *(She slaps Rust, Rust returns the slap. They scrap a second, break away, Rust has a fork from one of the tables.)*

RUST. Okay, you jealous cunt, now you mind your own business.

JUDY. *(Aware of the spectacle, past anger, hurt now.)* Why don't you mind ... you stay away from Terry.

RUST. Go slapping people around. I'm not interested in her!

JUDY. You stay away, I saw you!

RUST. You been asking for it all night!

JUDY. *We been together eleven months; you stay away!*

RUST. I'm not bothering her.

JUDY. *Go on....*

RUST. *(Throws the fork down.)* I'm leaving.

JOHN. *(Hangs up phone.)* You people sit down or get out.

RUST. I'm leaving, goddamnit.

JOHN. *(To all three.)* Come on, clear out. We can't have fights in here.

RUST. Just mind your own business!

TERRY. *(To John.)* Nothing's happening.

RUST. *(Storming out.)* She can pay.

TERRY. *(Calling to Rust.)* Get your coat.

RUST. I don't want it. *(Out to street corner.)*

JOHN. Now keep it down. That's all out of you two or outside.

TERRY. Bring another coffee over.

JUDY. *(Whimpering.)* I can't help it. *(They talk quietly in the booth.)*

DARLENE. What's wrong with them?

JOE. Huh? What?

DARLENE. Nothing. *(Phone rings. John answers it.)*

JOE. *(Trying to regain Darlene's attention.)* In a month or so I'll be making — well, really good money. Some guys like me, they got fellas working for them.

DARLENE. Sure. You know how to handle yourself. That's good. You remind me of this guy I knew in Chicago. Cotton. He knew how to handle himself.

RAKE. *(On the corner. To Rust.)* Aren't you cold?

RUST. No.

RAKE. You'll catch cold.

JOHN. *(At the phone.)* I'll see. I don't know.

RAKE. You're gonna catch pneumonia.

RUST. Just mind your own business, okay?

JOE. Yeah, well, you learn quick enough. I'll be making really good money. You have to be careful, of course.

DARLENE. Well, who doesn't?

JOE. You'll be all right.

RAKE. *(Rust has said something to him quietly.)* I can't go in there either.

JOHN. *(Comes to the side of Joe.)* Telephone. Sounds like one of Chuckles' fellows. Perry, I think.

JOE. Yeah? Tell him I'll be back in an hour or so.

JOHN. Okay. Don't take calls here — I told you before.

JOE. I didn't ask him to call me here. I'm not going to talk to him here. You know that.

JOHN. Okay.

JOE. *(To John.)* Okay. *(To Darlene.)* Besides, the fellow I'm tying in with — Chuckles. That was a friend of his. You don't cross him. You don't cross Chuckles.

KAY. Toast me a muffin.

JOHN. Toasted muffin.

JOE. You don't say yes today and say no tomorrow.

DARLENE. Yeah. I gotta go back over to the hotel. *(She gets up.)*

JOE. I thought you were working.

DARLENE. Working?

JOE. You know.

DARLENE. I thought I'd get to bed and kinna look around the neighborhood tomorrow and see if there's anything open.

JOE. Job? *(He gets up.)*

DARLENE. Or something. If anything's open. You have to live.

JOE.   Yeah.

DARLENE.   Do you want to walk me across the street? I'd like you to.

JOE.   What are you, a little old lady or something? Sure I will; protection. *(He pays.)*

DARLENE.   I mean if you're not doing anything.

JOE.   No, that's okay.

DARLENE.   I won't let you miss your ten-o'clock appointment.

JOE.   Screw that. Martin would wait all night. *(Exit. Dim almost out on café interior. Patrons inside walk to the front of the café and stand in a line across stage, back to the audience, forming a "wall." There is a space about four feet wide at the center of the wall, forming a doorway. Joe and Darlene walk down the wall slowly.)*

DARLENE.   I haven't seen the neighborhood at daytime yet.

JOE.   Neither has anybody else.

DARLENE.   I'll bet.

KAY.   *(From the café, distantly.)* Scramble two with bacon, John.

DARLENE.   It's getting cold.

JOE.   Yeah.

DARLENE.   There was snow last night.

JOE.   Was there?

DARLENE.   Not much. It didn't stick. Just a little. It's too early for snow. *(She walks inside the doorway and turns. He is outside.)*

JOE.   Yeah, you'd think so.

DARLENE.   Look, I don't want you to be late for your meeting, if you're meeting someone.

JOE.   It isn't important. What do you have in mind?

DARLENE.   I don't know. Do you want to come up? You can. I'd like for you to. You know. If you want to.

JOE.   Yeah, I'd like that. *(Rake leaves his place in the wall and comes toward the audience.)* I been thinking about just that for the last hour.

DARLENE.   Me too, really. *(They go through the "door," out of sight behind the "wall" of people.)*

JOHN.   *(From the café.)* You're sure as hell not going to make any money like that! *(The "wall" moves to close the doorway behind them.)*

RAKE.   *(To the audience.)* You travel around. I mean hustlers

38

travel around, after all they follow the sun, staying where the weather's warm. In New York, north, you know, when it's hot here. And in the winter they begin to drift down toward Miami Beach so it's warm. And out to California. All around. You hear a lot about Miami Beach but you don't hear that it's winter quarters for about half the hustlers in the country. I guess they don't advertise that — but the johns know it. A hustler tries to keep where it's warm. I don't know if it's because of warm weather and all or whether they just try to keep up a good tan, you know? What the hell, it's healthy. But you travel around and you start seeing differences in people. In the way people act from one place to another. Like in New York — the main difference between people in Chicago and New York is in New York everyone carries an umbrella. If it's the least bit cloudy you can depend on it, every goddamn plumber or electrician or construction worker or executive in New York carries an umbrella. It's just the way they think. They don't think about it. But see, Chicago, there it's this symbol or something. See in Chicago you're never going to see a construction worker carrying one of those narrow little rolled-up rapier kind of umbrellas. Or any other kind. It's unmasculine, see. They won't have it. In New York, sure; but in Chicago, not on your life. Fairies and old women, some, not many, carry umbrellas when it's really cloudy. But everyone else stays clear of that sort of thing. *(Pause.)* Consequently they get rained on a lot in Chicago. *(The "wall" disperses. People move off and back to the café, in every direction. There has been a bed set up behind the wall. Joe is in undershorts. He sits on the edge of the bed, then lies back, propped up on his elbow. Darlene has just slipped on a half-slip and bra. She stands over the bed for a moment. Then moves away a bit. The scene should be dimly lit. Rake walks off.)*

DARLENE. *(A little breathless.)* Oh, Lord. I'm all over sweat — perspiration. So are you. Look at you. Do you want a cigarette? How about that? *(Joe remains uninterested in her throughout this scene; quite remote.)*

JOE. Sure.

DARLENE. Jesus. *(She hands him a package of cigarettes and matches.)* Here you are, baby. *(Walking away.)* Let me get a towel. I feel like I'd gone for a swim. I'm wet and all, but I mean, my legs and arms weigh a ton; I just feel like I'd been swimming for hours.

I'll get a towel or something, how's that? *(Joe lights a cigarette.)* I thought I'd swipe this towel when I move, when I get an apartment of my own. It's got the name of the hotel across it. I thought that'd be funny; hanging in a regular bathroom. *(She dries her neck and arms on the towel.)* Oh, that's more like it. Here, let me. You're perspiring like a maniac.

JOE.   Throw it over.

DARLENE.   Here. *(She rubs his belly.)*

JOE.   Come on!

DARLENE.   It's not going to hurt you. *(She starts to dry his chest and face, Joe pulls back.)*

JOE.   Come on, Darlene. For Chris' sake! *(Pushing her gently away.)* For Chris' sake! *(He takes the towel.)*

DARLENE.   What? You take it then. Where did you put the cigarettes?

JOE.   Over here.

DARLENE.   *(Artificially gay, goes to them.)* Oh, swell. Lord. What time are you supposed to see that guy?

JOE.   What guy?

DARLENE.   I don't know. The guy that you're supposed to see. I don't know his name.

JOE.   Oh, for Chris' sake, I told you, Martin hangs around that corner all night long. If I miss him at ten he's around at eleven. It isn't important. He'll be there. He's a junkie.

DARLENE.   Looks to me like you all hang around there all night.

JOE.   Well it's an important place around here.

DARLENE.   You made it sound so mysterious.

JOE.   I don't have to answer to him. That's for damn sure. *(He puts his shirt and pants on, bragging.)* Look, you want to know something? You want to know something? I knew what I was doing. I keep a sharp lookout for myself, you don't have to worry about that. I watch people and size them up. And this guy Chuckles you heard me mention?

DARLENE.   Yeah?

JOE.   The guy who had someone call me back at the café. Now, this guy is probably the most important pusher — he doesn't push himself, but he supplies — and you don't screw around with him.

I got in touch with Chuckles a while back and told him I wanted to get cut in. Make some dough around the neighborhood. Hell, he'd been watching me for weeks. Months! And we made this deal. He gave — not give! — Chuckles never gave anyone the time of day. But he loaned — on credit — you know? He loaned me about a hundred dollars' worth of stuff....

DARLENE.   What kind of....

JOE.   Dope. Heroin. I told you....

DARLENE.   What do you do with it? You sell it to that guy?

JOE.   I sell it now and make twice or more profit. All I give him is his hundred. But see there's this — it's not this once only. If you're in with this guy like I wanted to be, you're in for a while. And chances are, like almost everyone you'll get picked up. A guy just starting runs all the risks. You can be about *so* clever. But once I sell that stuff — see, I'm in up to my throat. Hell, I'm in already. You don't butt out on Chuckles. You don't just carry it around.

DARLENE.   You don't sound very pleased about it.

JOE.   He loaned it to me for twenty-four hours, you know? And they been up a long time now. Day before yesterday. I just can't think straight on it. You don't cross him, though.

DARLENE.   I guess not, but if you think it's too dangerous....

JOE.   The sentence for pushing *H* is about thirty years! Hell, I'm the same as in with Chuckles already.

DARLENE.   I thought you just was. But if you don't want to be, you could talk with....

JOE.   *(Getting up.)* Christ!

DARLENE.   No, really. I've always felt if people just talked about their problems they can always work something out....

JOE.   Yeah, sure. What time is it?

DARLENE.   I don't know. Let's see.

JOE.   You want to call down and ask the desk?

DARLENE.   No. I have a wristwatch, I'm not that poor.

JOE.   What time is it?

DARLENE.   Well, I'm trying to read it, it's small! It's one-thirty.

JOE.   Christ! Oh, Christ! *(The people who have left the stage begin to drift in in the background, occasionally crossing in front.)*

FICK.   Hey, hey, Tig?

41

TIG.   Sure, don't even ask. Any time. Christ. *(Takes a cigarette and gives it to Fick.)*

DARLENE.   Why, do you have to go somewhere?

FICK.   *(Badly wetting and destroying the end of the cigarette.)* God, look at me slobber all over it. I'm a mess. Jesus.

JOE.   Jesus. *(He puts on his jacket.)*

DARLENE.   Do you have to go somewhere?

JOE.   Yeah. I'll see you tomorrow or if you come back tonight.

FICK.   I'm such a damn slob. Look at that. I'll get it though. *(Wanders back into café. Joe goes into the café. Darlene exits. The bed is removed. Lights up on café; very late at night. Ann is considerably more disheveled. As lights go up the first rock 'n 'roll song blasts out of the juke - box. John immediately reaches under the counter and turns it down.)*

TIG.   Hey, that's my song.

JOHN.   *(Over, to Joe as he enters.)* Martin was looking for you, Joe.

JOE.   Let him look. When?

JOHN.   God, I don't know; hours ago. Chuckles called you on the phone.

JOE.   *He* did? *(Shrugs.)* Coffee. What did you tell him?

JOHN.   I told him you left early.

JOE.   *(With a swagger.)* What does he want with me?

JOHN.   *(Knowingly.)* Yeah, I wonder, huh.

JOE.   How'd you get it so quiet in here?

JOHN.   Wait ten minutes. It'll be a madhouse. We had a dish-washer walk out.

JOE.   I never knew you had one.

ANN.   *(Entering.)* Coffee, okay, John?

JOHN.   Coffee for teacher.

ANN.   Oh, can it. Did you see that john? That last one?

JOHN.   See who?

ANN.   That fellow I took up.

JOHN.   No.

JOE.   Naw.

ANN.   God, was he sick.

JOHN.   You get all kinds, huh?

ANN.   All kinds and varieties.

JOHN.   How much was he worth?

ANN.   Fifteen. What the hell. You seen Sam? He's not been

42

around?

JOHN.   Your boyfriend? No.

ANN.   God, was he sick. Hey this guy last night — you should have seen him. He had a roll of bills, I've never seen anything like it. He owns some gas stations around — three or four and he'd just made the rounds and collected from them. He must have had six or eight hundred. And I'm feeding him booze and walking the floor trying to figure some way of getting it and he's getting ready to leave. And I keep talking about everything I can think of. Pulling him back. God, I'll bet he thought he'd got hold of an eager demented whore for sure. I nearly went nuts. Kept him in the room for an hour trying to think of some way to get it.

FICK.   *(To Tig in the back booth.)* You notice how cold it's getting?

JOHN.   Can't you stick to an honest living?

FICK.   Bet it snows. Me with no goddamned overcoat.

ANN.   Ha. He must have had six hundred. *(Pause.)*

FICK.   Goddamn.

ANN.   What the hell, who needs it? *(To Joe.)* What are you so quiet about anyway?

JOE.   Can't I be quiet?

ANN.   Sit over there like the bird that caught the cat.

JOE.   Can't I be quiet?

ANN.   No. Oh, hell. *(Gets up. At the back a Stranger, who has entered, gets up to pay his check.)* Oh, hell. Hell, hell, hell, hell, hell. *(Wanders out.)*

STRANGER.   *(To Joe.)* You Joe Conroy?

JOE.   Who are you?

STRANGER.   Are you Conroy?

JOE.   What are you? Some kind of cop or something?

STRANGER.   You pretty big around here?

JOE.   Who, me?

STRANGER.   You must be thinking you're pretty hot stuff around here.

JOE.   Hey, John, could I have cream with this, huh?

STRANGER.   You don't screw around with Chuckles; you don't cross Chuckles, Conroy. You ought to know that.

JOE.   What's that?

STRANGER.   You're a little late, and we understand. But business is business. So we'll have to have interest on the little loan.

JOE. Like what?

STRANGER. Like a hundred a day — every day you're late. Man, that's sad news. You're due to lose money at that rate, you know? *(Exits.)*

JOE. I'm not crossing nobody. Beginning when? Hey. *(Pause for a second.)* Hey, John. You know that guy?

JOHN. *(From the far end of the counter, looks up.)* No. Never saw him, don't think.

JOE. I think he's some kind of cop.

BOB. *(Entering with Tim.)* Yeah, yeah, yeah; whatta you think, whatta you think? Hey, John, we'll take a booth — coffee and we'll leave, okay?

JOHN. Fifty cents a person minimum.

BOB. Come on. Whatta you thinking about?

TIG. Hey, buddy.

BOB. Whatta you thinking?

JOHN. Fifty cents.

TIM. Since when?

JOHN. Since year one. Look, do I own the place or do I work here? I work here.

BOB. *(To Tig.)* Spare me a dollar till tomorrow morning, okay? I gotta pay someone before he —

TIG. I got no dollar. *(Lights begin to fade on the scene.)*

DOPEY. *(To Rake and Ernesto on the corner.)* It's here, right? This is it.

RAKE. No, God. Not yet.

JOHN. Sit somewhere.

BOB. Come on, tomorrow morning.

DOPEY. It is, go on, man; get it there.

RAKE. *(Pushing him back.)* Come on.

FICK. Damn, is it getting cold, man? Do you know what happened, Tig? To me? You know why I'm so mussed up? Did I tell you?

BOB. Just a minute. We'll take a booth, okay?

FICK. I told you, huh.

JOHN. Fifty cents a person.

BOB. Oh, for Chris' sake.

FICK. Do I, Tig? Do I?

TIG.   Do you what, Fick? I don't know what you're talking about.

RAKE.   *(Under his breath to Ernesto and Dopey.)* Okay, this is it. *(The lights are very dim on café. Ernesto, Rake, and Dopey come forward [Downstage C.] to audience.)*

ERNESTO.   We got this song here; we do this song.

DOPEY.   Read it.

RAKE.   I'll say it first, so you know the words or you couldn't make it out.

DOPEY.   It's a round.

RAKE.   It's a round and you can't understand the words if you don't know them.

DOPEY.   And the name is — see....

ERNESTO.   It's about us.

RAKE.   Yeah. The name is — see it's us; this is our song about us.

DOPEY.   We stand around on the corner all night, see, and don't do nothing.

RAKE.   You know, with our hands in our pockets like. Come on, Bob; you're in this — Tim, come on. *(Tim and Bob come to the group.)*

BOB.   What's up?

RAKE.   *(To Bob.)* Wake up!

ERNESTO.   *(Over.)* And the name is "Men on the Corner." Fellows on the corner, like that.

RAKE.   *(Ready to read the words from a piece of paper that he has taken from his pocket.)* Okay.

ERNESTO.   *(To audience.)* I'm not in it. *(Goes into the café.)*

RAKE.   It's this round. This is just the words:

> THEY LAUGH AND JAB
> CAVORT AND JUMP
> AND JOKE AND GAB
> AND GRIND AND BUMP.

DOPEY.   *(Quickly.)* See? It's us.

RAKE.

> THEY FLIP A KNIFE
> AND TOSS A COIN
> AND SPEND THEIR LIFE
> AND SCRATCH THEIR GROIN.

45

THEY PANTOMIME
A STANDING SCREW
AND PASS THE TIME
WITH NOUGHT TO DO.

THEY SWING, THEY SWAY
THIS CHEERFUL CREW,
WITH NOUGHT TO SAY
AND NOUGHT TO DO.

(Dopey begins the round as soon as Rake is finished, followed by Tim and Bob and Rake in that order. The melody is shockingly gentle; rocking; easy; soft; lilting.)

They laugh and jab ca-vort and jump and joke and gab and grind and bump.They

flip a knife and toss a coin and spend their life and scratch their groin.They

pan-to-mime a stand-ing screw and pass the time with nought to do. They

swing, they sway this cheer-ful crew with nought to say and nought to do.

(In the background with a minimum of extraneous movement the people in the café silently lift every stick of furniture, the "set," about three feet off the ground and turn the set — as a turntable would — walk the set in a slow circle until it is facing the opposite direction from the beginning. They set the furniture down in place and sit. The round ends.)

DOPEY. *(As the last line of the round is sung.)* See, the words of this one make some sense anyway. If you read the other one — the rock'n'roll at the beginning of the show — it would sound like this: y-ooo, y-ooo, yackie-yackie do, y-ooo, y-ooo, yackie, yackie....

ERNESTO. *(To Dopey.)* Come on.

DOPEY. "What would I do yackie, yackie do, y-ooo, y-ooo....

ERNESTO. Let s go.

DOPEY. Isn't that a bitch?

RAKE. Come on. Bob, you and Tim go on back. *(Tim and Bob enter café as Dopey and Rake go back to the street corner. To the audience.)* We'll see you. *(Lights up in the café.)*

FICK. You didn't see it, Tig; I tell you they had me pinned, man. Down in this hall-thing. Four or five big black cats, they must have been huge....

DARLENE. *(Entering the café.)* Hi, Joe.

JOE. Hi.

DARLENE. Couldn't sleep. I thought you might be here.

JOE. Sure. *(All of Fick's dialogue in this scene is over Darlene and Joe's scene, as a background. Very soft at first here. Fick is in the back of the café. To Tig who is not listening. Fick's dialogue is continuous.)*

FICK. I mean, big, strong fellows; fighters. They pushed me into this doorway. Right into the door, and down this hall and back into this dark place there in the hall there.

DARLENE. What's wrong?

JOE. Whatta you mean?

DARLENE. You look like something was wrong is all.

JOE. Do I?

DARLENE. What's wrong? You can tell me.

JOE. Nothing, goddamnit. Come on — you come in here and in three seconds flat you start telling me I'm crazy or something.

DARLENE. I didn't say anything like that.

JOE. Hell you didn't.

FICK. See, they thought I had a bottle on me, and I said I don't drink, and they didn't know I was high, you know. And they're standing over me and they feel around and see I don't have any money on me and I said, shit, man, you think I walk around with money? I mean, look at me now, do I look like I carry money around with me? I don't have any money on me.

DARLENE. I just asked. Hell! Look at you!

JOE. Don't look at me then.

DARLENE. What's bugging you anyway?

JOE. Nothing. Damnit. Darlene. *(Nicer.)* What the hell am I

47

going to do with you anyway?

DARLENE. *(Nicer.)* I don't know. I swear I don't. You let me know when you come up with something, though, you hear?

JOE. Yeah. I'll think of something. *(Pause in their conversation.)*

FICK. I get four dollars, I shoot it, man it's all I can afford. About twenty dollars a day, man, most days I don't even know where it came from, 'cause I'm high, man, and I don't remember, I can't think. And they start roughing me up and I said, man, you got the wrong boy. Why don't you rough up someone your own size?

JOE. You want a cup of coffee?

DARLENE. Sure. Why not. John? I won't sleep now, anyway. *(Pause.)* Did you get back in time to see that Martin?

JOE. Oh, Christ. What the hell difference does it make? I told you I don't owe him nothing.

DARLENE. I didn't know. I take it from that you didn't get back in time.

JOE. What business is it of yours, anyway?

DARLENE. Well, I just wondered. For Christ's sake. If you can't even be civil.

FICK. I mean even if I was a big cat, see, I'm small, but even if I was a big cat I wouldn't go roughing up people like that. They fairly gave me hell, and beat the tar out of me. I just balled up in the hall there and didn't move, I mean, if I get up they're going to get at my face and all, and I just balled up and had to take it.

JOE. Well, if you have to nose into everybody's business.

DARLENE I don't give a good goddamn if you saw him or not. Or Chuckles even.

JOE. Then why the hell did you bother to ask?

DARLENE. Forget it. Christ. Excuse me for living.

JOE. Just keep your nose in your own business. You have business of your own to worry about. Darlene, for Christ's sake.

FICK. 'Cause I couldn't get even one good punch in at them. I couldn't get one good punch at them. I mean, look at me, I'm weak as a kitten. What would you expect, I started shooting *H* when I was about thirteen. And hell, that's a long time ago now; I mean I wasn't a tough kid or nothing like that, but I could protect myself, you know, I could spar around, but Christ I can't even see anything half the time, I can't follow things around you know and they're kicking me around the hallway there. *(Tig starts to get up, sits back down.)*

DARLENE.   Pardon me for living.

JOE.   Go get laid. You can't mind your own business. You come in here and....

DARLENE.   Jesus. Just forget it.

JOE.   Okay. It's forgotten. *(Pause.)*

FICK.   No, don't go away now, listen to this, just listen to me now. See these guys were kicking me around and I can't do nothing. But what I'm saying, if I could get a couple of big guys, you know, a few big guys, you know, a few big guys and go up there, go back there.

DARLENE.   Christ! *(Pause.)*

JOE.   You want coffee?

DARLENE.   I don't know.

JOE.   Suit yourself.

DARLENE.   Yeah. Okay John?

JOHN.   Got it.

JOE.   Christ.

DARLENE.   Are you in trouble? Be serious now.

JOE.   Yes. Damnit, there. You feel better now?

FICK.   I couldn't do nothing myself, I mean, I just laid there, man. But if I could just get a couple of big guys, a couple of fighters and go back there. No, don't run off, I'm not talking about you, but you're big fellows, you could look big. See I know these mothers; I seen them around here all the time. And they know I don't have any bread, they know that. *(Tig moves to a different seat. Fick continues as if Tig were still there.)*

DARLENE.   Is it serious?

FICK.   But with a couple of fellows, fighters, they'd run like hell, they wouldn't start nothing, you'd see.

JOE.   Yes.

FICK.   They'd run like a couple of scared mothers. I mean we wouldn't have to do nothing or nothing, they'd just turn tail and get the hell out of there.

DARLENE.   Are you going to work for him?

JOE.   I don't have much of a choice. One of his friends — one

49

that I'd never seen before — paid me a visit here to inform me I'd owe Chuckles a hundred bucks a day interest till I paid him off. Now are you happy?

FICK.   See, they'd think I had friends, see, and they'd know not to fuck with me any more, as soon as they saw I had a couple of friends they'd not mess around with me, you know what I mean?

DARLENE.   You can't get money like that, can you? Can you? What are you going to do, Joe?

JOE.   I don't know yet! I don't know. What, yet. I gotta think. *(They sit quietly, looking up out toward the street.)*

FICK.   I mean, I was just walking down the street and they came up on me like they was important, and they start pushing me around, you know. And they pushed me into this alley, not an alley, but this hallway and back down the end of that to this dark place at the end of the hallway and they start punching at me, and I just fell into this ball on the floor so they couldn't hurt me or nothing. But if I came down there with a couple of fighters, a couple of guys, like my friends, it wouldn't have to be you or anything, but just a couple or three guys, big guys, like walking down the street, you know. Just so they could see I got these buddies here. See I'm on *H*, I mean, I'm flying and I gotta talk man, but I'm serious now; just a few guys and they'd leave me be, maybe, because they'd think I had these buddies that looked after me, you know; 'cause I — you know — they kicked me up, if I wasn't on *H*, man, they'd be pains all through me — you know — walking down the street by myself — I start looking around and wondering who's out there gonna mess me up, you know. I get scared as hell, man, walking down around here, I mean, I can't protect myself or nothing man. You know what I mean? You know what I mean? You know what I mean? You know? I mean if I had these couple of big buddies — fighters — you — you know — if I had a couple of guys — like — big guys — that — you know, there's like nothing — I could — like, if you walked around with these buddies, I mean you could do, man — you could do anything.... *(Long pondering pause. He looks to everyone one at a time. No one moves. He turns and looks at Babe. She raises her head as if to speak and very slowly looks back down to the counter.)*

DOPEY. *(On the corner. Turns to audience. Clearly.)* We'll call an intermission here. *(Curtain.)*

ACT TWO

*Early evening. Only Frank, Ann, Judy, and Terry are in the café.
Ann is the only person seated at the counter.*

DARLENE. *(Enters the café. She sits a few stools from Ann.)* Could I
have a coffee, please?

FRANK. *(In a rather good mood.)* Sure, miss.

DARLENE. John isn't on yet, huh? He come on about seven?

FRANK. Yeah.

DARLENE. And I think maybe — what's the little cupcake? Are
those chocolate all through?

FRANK. White. Chocolate frosting.

DARLENE. Oh. No. Nothing else, I guess. I'm not really hungry.
*(She looks toward Ann. Darlene pours a great deal of milk into the
coffee.)*

FRANK. Watch that milk — all that's not good for you. *(You
have the feeling he's more worried about the price of milk.)*

DARLENE. It isn't?

FRANK. It'll make you fat. *(He walks to the far end of the counter.)*

DARLENE. Oh, that's one thing I don't worry much about. *(She
looks toward Ann who is drinking coffee and smoking a cigarette, looking
out the window in a half-dream.)* Isn't your name Ann? *(Pause. No
reaction. Ann probably hasn't heard her.)* Ann? I thought, if you're
busy or....

ANN. *(Turns to her. Does not recognize her at first.)* Yes?

DARLENE. I don't know many people around the neighborhood yet. I've seen you around. A friend of mine knows you real
well. Joe knows you, I think. *(Frank sits at one of the booths, reading
a newspaper.)*

ANN. Joe? Conroy? Chuckles' fellow? Or is he?

DARLENE. I don't — short — but not too short. Real cute —

sexy; dark hair. I don't think he's Chuckles' fellow, but he knows him, I believe.

ANN.   Conroy. God yes, I know Joe.

DARLENE.   Isn't that terrible, I forgot his last name. I just blanked out.

ANN.   Conroy.

DARLENE.   Yes, I know. I remember it now.

ANN.   Sure. I've seen you with Joe, I know now.

DARLENE.   I'm Darlene.

ANN.   Fine.

DARLENE.   Joe said you came to New York to be a teacher.

ANN.   Oh, God.

DARLENE.   Didn't you?

ANN.   Who remembers?

DARLENE.   And you're from Nebraska. I'm from Chicago, so that's not far off.

ANN.   Minnesota.

DARLENE.   *(Puzzled for a moment — smiles.)* Illinois.

ANN.   I'm from Minnesota. You're from Chicago.

DARLENE.   Oh. Minnesota. I said something else, didn't I? *(Pause.)* I been here about a month, I guess. He — Joe — talked about you a lot.

ANN.   He must have.

DARLENE.   Oh, it was all good! *(Realizes it couldn't have been good. Embarrassed hesitation.)* I saw you this afternoon.

ANN.   Me?

DARLENE.   I was up early for a change; I had to go down to Port Authority and get some things I'd left there. You were walking down uh — uh — over toward that church; the whichever one — I don't know — there's a market there and a bakeshop.

ANN.   I don't know.

DARLENE.   Yes, you do. You were with this guy. Probably your boyfriend. Real big fellow.

ANN.   Boyfriend for the next fifteen minutes probably — Oh, no! That was Sam. That *is* my boyfriend. If you can call it that. He dragged me out of bed to look at a TV set some bum friend of his mopped from a *PR* apartment. Ratty old contraption. He couldn't get either one of us focused.

DARLENE. *(Has been listening too intently, too amused.)* Huh?

ANN. Some clunk friend of his was trying to fence a bum set for twenty-five bucks. I dragged him down to some store and bought a new one.

DARLENE. Really? That's wonderful.

ANN. He didn't like it, of course. There wasn't anything that needed to be done on it. Tinkered with. He didn't want to watch it unless he could conquer it first. His room is one solid mass of parts and tubes and coils and wires and various masculine symbols like that. Of course, *he* is one solid mass of — but that's another conversation altogether. You're from Chicago. I went to Chicago when I was about four, I think.

DARLENE. Really? Yeah, I grew up there. It's not like New York at all.

ANN. Yeah.

DARLENE. I know what you mean about radio parts and nuts and bolts and everything. That's funny, the way you put it. *(Pause.)* Oh, I like New York all right, I guess. It's like a whole different place, you know.

ANN. I imagine.

DARLENE. I mean back home is like a small town compared to here.

ANN. For me, too. *(Martin enters café.)*

DARLENE. You're from Minnesota?

ANN. Ashville, Minnesota.

MARTIN. Pardon me. Ann. Right?

ANN. Yes?

MARTIN. *(Mumbles.)* I thought so; I wondered, there's this guy I've....

ANN. Speak up, baby, I can't hear you.

MARTIN. I said, there's this guy, I know he comes around here.

ANN. Who's that?

MARTIN. I don't know, I know I heard he was around here, I've seen him around. Spanish fellow, dark....

ANN. I don't think I can help you on that one, there's a *lot* of Spanish guys floating around here. *(She starts to turn away.)*

MARTIN. He's a Colombian guy; dresses very smart.

ANN. Are you talking about Xavier?

DARLENE.   That's who I was gonna say, *Xavier.*

MARTIN.   Yes, yes, that's him; that's him.

ANN.   Sure, everybody knows Xavier.

MARTIN.   Have you seen him around today?

ANN.   I don't think so.

MARTIN.   *(Overlapping.)* Has he been in here today?

ANN.   Not that I know of.

MARTIN.   A Colombian guy, very smart dress —

ANN.   Yeah, I know who you mean. *(To Darlene.)* Sorry, you were saying it's —

MARTIN.   Do you know where he'd be; or where he lives or anything?

ANN.   No, I'm afraid I don't.

DARLENE.   He's been around this week, though. With *Xavier* you never know when you're going to see him.

ANN.   He runs around a lot.

DARLENE.   He says I'll be right back and you won't see him for a month sometimes.

ANN.   Sorry. *(Pause.)*

MARTIN. Yeah. *(Pause.)*

DARLENE.   *(To Ann.)* That guy that you were with, the tall —

MARTIN.   *(Overlapping, conversational level.)* You don't suppose that he'll be in right away?

ANN.   I tell you what, you could undoubtedly catch him later on this evening; why don't you come back?

MARTIN.   Yeah. I just wanted to see him about something.

ANN.   Well, if it's important I could —

MARTIN.   No, no. It's not important.

ANN.   If I see him do you want me to tell him to stick around?

MARTIN.   No. No, that's okay. I'll probably run into him, you know, his evening. Thank you.

ANN.   Sure.

FRANK.   You want something?

MARTIN.   No, no, thanks.

FRANK.   Coffee or something. It's getting cold out.

MARTIN.   *(Leaving.)* No, I'll be back, no thanks.

DARLENE.   What was the fellow's name again?

ANN.   Him? I don't know, I've seen him around.

DARLENE.   No, the tall guy; you know, that I saw you with?

ANN.   Sam?

DARLENE.   Yeah. You're not married to him, are you?

ANN.   God, no.

DARLENE.   *(Laughs.)* I know what you mean. That's funny. *(Pause.)* Those two that always sit around in here, you know; the dark headed one and she's got a little baby? Are they married? Or do you know?

ANN.   I don't know. No one knows. I don't imagine, but they'd probably tell you they were.

DARLENE.   It's a cute little baby, really. I don't know if I'd bring him here at all hours of the day and night like that if it was mine, though.

ANN.   Well, some people would give anything to look respectable.

DARLENE.   *(Pause.)* I know one thing: I sure feel like you do about marriage. I mean, I just don't know. Like you said. I know this guy I used to go with — when I first got a room of my own, up on Armitage Street? Do you know that part of Chicago?

ANN.   No. But then I was only four.

DARLENE.   Oh. Well, most of the streets run either east and west or up and down, you know — one or the other. But some of them kinna cut across all the others — Armitage Street does, and some of the other real nice ones. Fullerton Street does. *(I don't know if it's important, but Fullerton Street does not. In other words, Darlene rather prefers the vivid to the accurate.)* And they're wider, you know, with big trees and all, and there are all of these big old lovely apartment buildings, very well taken care of, with little lawns out front and flower boxes in the windows and all. You know what I mean? And the rents, compared to what they try to sock you with here. The rents are practically nothing — even in this neighborhood. *(Pause.)* My apartment was two flights up, in the front. It was so cute, you'd have loved it. They had it all done over when I moved in. I had three rooms. And let's see — there was just a lovely big living room that looked out onto Armitage Street and a real cute little kitchen and then the bedroom — that looked out onto a garden in the back and on the other side of the garden was Grant Park — or some park, I never did know the name it had. But there were kids that I just loved playing out in this park all the time. And then I had this little bathroom, a private bath. I had — it was funny — I had a collection — you know practically everybody collects something....

ANN.   Yeah, I know what you mean.

DARLENE.   *(Laughs.)* No, not like that! I collected towels, if you must know. You know, from all the big hotels — Of course, I didn't get very many of them myself, but friends of mine, every time they went anywhere always brought me back a big bath towel or hand towel or face towel with some new name across it. I'll swear, I never bought one towel in all the time I lived there! It was funny, too, it looked real great in a regular bathroom like that; these hotel names. Everyone just loved it. My favorite one was — from this — oh, this real elegant hotel — what was it's — I don't even remember the name any more I had so many of them. Anyway, the apartment, in that neighborhood and all, cost me practically nothing compared to what they want for a place not half as good in New York. And I lived there, and this guy I was going with, you know, that asked me to marry him? He lived across the hall. He moved into the apartment next to mine. Really, Ann, you should have seen him. He was slow, everything he did, and quiet; he hardly ever talked at all. You had to just pump him to get him to say the time of day. And he had white hair — nearly white; they used to call him Cotton — he told me — when he was in Alabama. That's where he's from. He was living in the apartment next to mine and we were always together, and there just wasn't any difference between his place and mine. We should have only been paying for one rent. Half of his stuff was in my place and half vice versa. He used to get so pissed off when I'd wash things out and hang them up in his bathroom or in the kitchen and all. You know, over the fire there. But we were always together — and we finally decided to get married — we both did. And all our friends were buying rice and digging out their old shoes. Cotton — he worked in a television factory, RCA, I believe, but I couldn't be sure. That's why I started thinking about him when you said this Sam had electrical parts all over the apartment. Old Cotton had, I'll swear, the funniest temperament I ever saw. If he got mad — *(Almost as though angry.)* — he wouldn't argue or anything like that, he'd just walk around like nothing was wrong only never say one word. Sometimes for two or three days. And that used to get me so mad I couldn't stand it. Have you ever known anyone who did that?

ANN. Yeah, I know what you mean.

DARLENE. Just wouldn't talk at all, I mean. Not say one word for days.

ANN. It sounds familiar enough.

DARLENE. It used to just burn me up. And he knew it did, is what made it so bad. I'd just be so mad I could spit. And I'd say something like: *what's wrong, Cotton?* And just as easy as you please he'd reach over and light a cigarette and look out the window or something. Turn on the radio. I just wish I had the control to be like that because it is the most maddening thing you can possibly do to someone when they're trying to argue with you. I could do it for about five minutes, then I'd blow my stack. Oh, I used to get so damn mad at him. *Agh! (Pause.)* Course I make it sound worse than it was, 'cause he didn't act like that very often. Fortunately. But you never knew what was going to provoke him, I swear. It was just that we saw each other every hour of every day — you just couldn't get us apart. And when we decided to get married all our friends were so excited — of course, they'd been expecting it probably. But we were so crazy you'd never know what we were going to do. I know he used to set the TV so it pointed into the mirror, because there wasn't a plug-in by the bed and we'd lay there in bed and look at the mirror that had the TV reflected in it. Only everything was backwards. Writing was backwards. *(She laughs.)* Only, you know, even backwards, it was a better picture, it was clearer than if you was just looking straight at it.

ANN. Yeah. So did you?

DARLENE. Get married? Oh, Lord, it was such an *ordeal!* We got — now you have to know Cotton for this to be funny to you — but when he went for his blood test I nearly died laughing. He's got these real pale eyes and just no color, you know — a pink color all over him; absolutely the lightest-skinned person I've ever known who wasn't sickly or something. They called him an albino; you know what that is?

ANN. Yes.

DARLENE. It's a kind of horse. And Cotton's eyes were kinda pink and trying to be blue, so they came out a kind of lavender. You'd have thought he couldn't be a lighter color and be alive. And when the doctor stuck the needle in him, oh, Lord, he faded out like a dollar shirt. I've never seen anyone in my life get that white in three seconds flat. I don't mean he fainted or anything, but you should have seen him. He was so damn scared it was really great of him, because he didn't make a fuss or anything. I said, honey, do you want to sit down or something? And he just said, oh, no. Cotton wasn't weak either — he was tough as they make 'em. He was pale and all like I said, but he was strong as an ox and rough. He was always in some fight, beating the pants off someone or other. *(Chattier.)* We went to this doctor Lillian — a girlfriend of mine — went to when she thought she was pregnant, but she wasn't, thank God. And I think it was the following Saturday, the license office was only open till noon or one o'clock, I remember. And Cotton was supposed to work, but he got off; we went up to City Hall for our license. They're building a new building for City Hall in Chicago, or I think they are. I *hope* they are! They didn't have any air conditioning or anything — naturally, and of course it was in the middle of summer: July eleventh. On a Saturday. Anyway, this old building covers a whole block, right out to the sidewalk and it must be fifty years old. Everything is that old style of heavy old marble and gold spittoons everywhere. And you go — going to the marriage license place — you go up these real wide marble stairs about a block wide and sway-backed, you practically break your neck on them they're so worn down in the middle — and there's this hall upstairs somewhere with the door to the bureau at the far end and by the time we got there — and we didn't get there till about eleven — there must have been two hundred people up there waiting in line. Most of them couples waiting to get in for their license. There was this line — you've never seen anything like it. We got up to the top of the stairs and saw all these people in line and Cotton and me both said, Oh, my God! at the same time. And some of the kids who had come with us, I thought they'd just drop. You've never seen anything like it. I wish I could remember some of the things that our friends said about it, too, because they kept us in stitches all morning. *(Pause.)* God, you should have seen the people waiting there in line. It was hot and all. Of course this was Chicago, but I'll bet it'll be the same, or about the same everywhere. There was every size and shape and color a person you've ever seen or could hope to see. God, there was Puerto Ricans and whites and redheads and Negroes and redheaded Negroes; and a lot of people were chattering away in some jibberish language that nobody could understand. And kids you'd think was only about fourteen years of age and old people who must have been — one couple — must have been sixty if they were a day. You see everything. And this is hard to believe probably but you can go down to the New York City Hall and I'll bet it's the same there; I'll swear about twenty of the girls in line waiting for their marriage licenses were pregnant. Honest to God. It looked like the maternity ward in a hospital. And I mean real pregnant — six or seven months along — and I couldn't help thinking if this many are this pregnant this far along, I just wonder how many are three months or two months along and nobody can tell it.

And of course there were some mothers and fathers that had dragged along. If you ever want to see a trapped look in a boy's eyes — I mean, they were smiling, and talking all very seriously with their prospective fathers-in-law, all very man to man, standing beside their fat, ugly — really ugly, some of them — girlfriends, and in their eyes they were wondering how the hell they were going to get out of this one. And some of the girls were dressed up. Some of them were in jeans and had their hair in curlers and you'd just want to die looking at them — and then some of them were dressed to the teeth. Knee-length wedding gowns; you know; not expensive, but pretty and veils and the whole bit — a bunch of roses or gardenias or something and after they got their license they went around a kind of mezzanine railing to the Justice's office across the way. The Justice of the Piece's office some of the kids started calling it. That's the kind of thing they were saying all day. But if I was going to wear a dress like that to get married in, I know one thing: I wouldn't do it in his little office — you could look right across into the room and the carpet was worn all down — it was just a mess of a place. I couldn't even watch — I just bet they felt so foolish all dressed up like that with this noisy line outside and that stupid rug. But they seemed happy enough about it, I guess. You couldn't help wondering if the boys who were marrying the pregnant girls were really the fathers of the kids or not. And if the boys weren't wondering the same thing. I just hope that all the kids turned out for the mothers' sake to look exactly the spittin' image of their fathers.

And if this hot, messy, stupid crowd wasn't enough, with everyone crowding all over this hall: there was this guy, all fat and toothless, or nearly, and bald, who kept trotting down the line saying, "Stay up against the wall, now, give the boys room to get in. They got you up against the wall now; now you let them in!" And pretending what he'd said didn't have any dirty meaning at all. And laughing. Some of the fellows and the men — the fathers and all — laughed and carried on with him. I can't remember exactly what he said but it was like: "The quicker you get in the quicker you get it in." I mean he just wasn't funny at all. I thought Cotton was gonna bust him one. He just *served* to make everyone a little more nervous and jumpy than they were anyway. Everyone got so tired and just kept looking and everyone was so down. Naturally the girls who were pregnant were mostly just looking down at the hall floor, and they'd look up like nothing was wrong. I guess everyone just wanted to get the hell out of that building. I know I thought, *Christ, aren't we even moving? You know?* With, let's see, with Cotton and me there was two friends of his that I didn't know too well, and a girl friend of mine, so we weren't as bad off as the kids that had come down there alone. Not at first. We were talking and cutting up and all. And after a while you get so tired and exhausted you just stand there. And everyone was more stupid and ugly than you can imagine and Cotton got in one of his moods. You know: quiet as a stone statue or something and I tried to get him out of it. It was like he blamed *me* for all the waiting and all. And then when we finally got in, after creeping along all afternoon, there was three tables and after we got inside the room the line split into three lines and we went to one of the tables — and the guy who asked the questions — real crazy questions too, but I can't remember any of them now. I should, too, because they were such crazy questions. This guy was friendly and nice and

Cotton became hisself again, which was about time. Anyway that guy was nice and friendly, considering he'd been doing the same thing all morning with one couple after another. And all the guys joked kinna dirty, but friendly and we finally got the license and they had the certificate from the blood test and all; and we went back out to the kids that waited for us. They were sitting on the steps, just about to die it looked like. I don't know how they did it. But a lot of the couples were worse off than we were — there seemed like thousands of them still hanging around up there when we left. Elizabeth — that was the girlfriend of mine who came along, stood out on the front steps there with the license and read it out — every word. Out loud. And everyone was laughing and carrying on. Christ, they were a fun gang. They were about the most fun kids I've ever been with in my life. And let's see; we went for a drive, trying to cool off, I remember. And anyway, to make a long story short, we probably went to a drive-in movie, out somewhere. We were always doing that because Harold had his car. And when we got home I put the license on the dresser, stood it up so we could look at it. Cotton said if we'd all been getting two dollars an hour the thing was worth about thirty dollars, I'll bet. *(Pause.)* When had we decided to get *married?* I think at first we were going to do it the next day — Sunday, but we'd been out all night that night and by the time we got up that Sunday it must have been seven or eight o'clock in the evening. And then we were going to do it the next week. And, I don't know — something came up — one thing or another. Cotton was out a lot, but he still came over and all, and he still wanted to and so did I. I really did. I wanted to more than anything because he was about the greatest guy I'd ever met. And I don't know. I know one time when I was trying to straighten up the place — trying to get a little order out of my room, I put it in one of the dresser drawers and it finally got buried under a pile of stuff. I've got it though, I ran across it again when I was packing things together to come here. Hell, old Cotton had cut out months before that. He kept coming over for a long time, but I might not be able to tell when a guy isn't really interested in me at first — I mean if they just say they are, I believe them — I mean what else can you do? But I can sure as hell tell when they start losing interest. Not that you can do

63

anything about it. Old Cotton would give me a kiss and squeeze me once and slap me three or four times quick on the rump. And say, "Okay!" like I was dismissed or something. Like he had better things to run and do at that particular moment, or he had thoughts; like he was preoccupied at the moment. "Okay! Hop up!" Hop up. Good Lord.

But he hadn't chickened out of it — getting married — he just never got around to it. I've sometimes wished we just had gone out of town, out to Glen Ellyn, or somewhere at a Justice of the Peace, somewhere. You know. It just got to be such a mess we never even talked about it after a while, and the license got shuffled up with a lot of other things, and got a bend across it, all bent up. He was a nice guy, too. He moved on back South somewhere. Georgia, I think. Not Alabama, I know. And he'd had a lot of great friends, too. I liked them a lot. God, did we ever have some *times* together. The whole … gang of us. God. We used … to really have some … times together. *(The quartette is together at the back of the stage. They harmonize in a rock'n'roll wordless "Boo, bop, boo, bah, day, dolie, olie day" kind of rambling that gets louder and eventually takes over the scene. Frank has left; John is in the café now. Joe and Dopey and Rake have gone to the corner. David and Franny enter the café.)*

DAVID.   Hi, John; you got any coffee?

JOHN.   Sure.

FRANNY.   Two. *(Darlene looks in her purse for money.)*

ANN.   I'll get it.

DARLENE.   No, that's okay.

ANN.   It's okay. Sam couldn't possibly miss a quarter.

FRANNY.   Do you have a menu in this place? For Chris' sake. *(Xavier and Babe enter. Babe is not high but is so far gone that you couldn't tell it. She speaks very thickly and to the floor and it should be just barely possible to understand her. Their scene should be played on the street, some distance from the corner, very slowly.)*

JOHN.   *(To Franny.)* Hold it a minute. *(To Ann.)* Thanks. *(Ann and Darlene remain in the café for a moment.)*

XAVIER.   *(To Joe.)* Hey, friend.

JOE.   *Xavier!* What are you doing?

XAVIER.   Where was you yesterday?

JOE.   Oh, I was busy. Where you going?

XAVIER.   You want to come up?

JOE.   *(Looks at Babe, nods. Babe stares blankly at him.)* Where you going?

BABE.   Come on, Xavier.

XAVIER.   We're going up on the roof a minute.

RAKE.   *(From the other side, singing to himself.)* They laugh and jab, cavort, and jump! —

DOPEY.   Shut up. For Chris' sake.

RAKE.   What's wrong?

JOE.   No, I been up there. What for?

DOPEY.   You get on my nerves.

BABE.   *(To Xavier.)* Haven't you got one? A something?

XAVIER.   We've got to go on up. *(Ernesto joins Dopey and Rake.)*

BABE.   Come on. You have to have something. You used to have a cord or something, didn't you?

XAVIER.   Yeah, someone borrowed it, didn't give it back.

BABE.   *(Looks at Joe's belt.)* Uh, do you think I, would you.... *(Joe slips off his belt, rolls it up, and hands to Xavier.)*

ANN.   I just wonder where the fuck Sam's run off to.

BABE.   Good, great. That's thin, that's fine.

JOE.   I'll see you when you come down. Don't lose that.

XAVIER.   *(Rather shyly.)* Come on up.

JOE.   No, I'll see you when you come down. Don't lose that.

XAVIER.   I'll bring it right back. We'll see you.

JOE.   Yeah, look; I'm not staying around here long, I might be inside when you come down, okay?

XAVIER.   Sure, man. We'll be right back. You should come along.

JOE.   You go on. *(Xavier and Babe exit.)* Jesus, Xavier. *(The quartette sings the first four or five lines of "There Is a Balm in Gilead"* in the back, a jazzed-up version.)*

DARLENE.   *(Comes out of the café. Sees Joe and goes to him. Their scene is played on the street corner.)* Hi.

JOE.   Hi. You been calling over to your room for me?

DARLENE.   No, you said not to. Why, has the phone been ringing?

JOE.   Yeah. It's probably Chuckles. I don't imagine it took him much to discover who I was with the last few nights. You being new and all.

---

*See Special Note on Songs and Recordings on copyright page.

DARLENE. Almost everyone I've seen all day asked me where you was.

JOE. Yeah? What'd you say?

DARLENE. *(Smiles.)* I told them I thought you went to a movie.

JOE. Really? That's pretty good. That's funny. Say, you know Xavier?

DARLENE. Sure. Someone was looking for him.

JOE. I saw him. Pushing now. I'll bet he has been all along. He was with Babe.

DARLENE. Babe? Really? *(She has no idea what to say.)*

JOE. I'm not going to.

DARLENE. Not what?

JOE. I'm not going to. I decided not.

DARLENE. Really? Oh, God, I'm glad, Joe. Oh, I really am. How are you gonna do it?

JOE. I gotta think of some way to get these back to Perry or Chuckles. I'll just give him what he gave me and tell him I've changed my mind. *(Franny enters.)*

DARLENE. Oh, I'm glad. I really am. You'll do something else all right.

FRANNY. *(On the street opposite the corner.)* Hello, Ernesto. *(The quartette begins a very low, highly harmonized version of the hymn "Balm in Gilead"* that follows the tempo of Joe and Darlene's slow, rather dreamy scene.)*

DARLENE. Did you sleep till six?

ERNESTO. *(With deep insinuation, grabbing Franny around waist.)* — You like it?

FRANNY. I'm not really interested, no. *(As Tig joins Dopey, Franny, Rake, and Ernesto.)* Hi, Tig.

JOE. About six. I didn't get to bed till late.

DARLENE. I know.

TIG. *(With hand on crotch.)* You like it, Franny? You think you could use something?

FRANNY. I'll bet you think you're a man. Don't you know —

DARLENE. When are you going to see him?

FRANNY. — men don't dig boys? They sure don't dig fairies.

TIG. Depends on what it's worth to you.

JOE. I don't know. Soon as I can. I got to call him or something.

*See Special Note on Songs and Recordings on copyright page.

DARLENE. When did you decide?

FRANNY. You really think you're hot stuff, don't you?

TIG. How much is it worth to you?

JOE. Just a minute ago.

DARLENE. What'll you do?

JOE. Hell, there's a thousand things to do.

ANN. *(Exiting the café.)* Franny, you're stealing all my business. *(Group laughs.)*

DARLENE. Sure.

FRANNY. *(To Tig.)* You really think you're good enough to charge?

TIG. Five bucks an inch'll get me fifty, Franny?

FRANNY. Who from? Not me.

JOE. When did you wake up?

FRANNY. I'll charge you double.

DARLENE. Since about ten....

TIG. How much can you take?

FRANNY. As much as I need and want.

TIG. Put your money where your mouth is, sweetheart. *(Group laughs. Tig is very close to Franny.)*

DARLENE. I went down to the bus station. I had some clothes still in a locker there; I thought I'd never get them.

FRANNY. More than you got, sweetheart.

TIG. How do you know?

DOPEY. Watch it, Tig. *(His back is to the audience, hands in pockets.)*

ANN. *(Turns and goes back inside.)* Watch it, Franny; he'll take you up.

FRANNY. Come on, back off a little bit. I'm only human.

KAY. *(Entering café.)* Hi, John; I'm a little late.

JOHN. Hi, Kay; that's all right. *(Fick enters.)*

DARLENE. *(Over some of the above.)* The neighborhood isn't bad at all in the daytime. It's perfectly respectable.

JOE. Is it?

DARLENE. Well. Nearly.

RAKE. He can take care of himself.

FRANNY. I'll bet I could take care of him better.

TIG. You think you could take about half of that?

FRANNY. Half of what? I don't *see* anything.

RAKE. Watch that one, though, Tig. *(Group reaction.)*

ERNESTO. No lie, Tig.

DARLENE. The people look like anyone else. Almost.

JOE. Almost. That's funny.

TIG. You think you can take about ten bucks' worth, real quick-like?

FICK. *(Inside the café.)* Hey, John? Am I frostbitten? Look at my ears.

JOHN. What?

DOPEY. Why don't you take us all on, huh?

RAKE. Game for that?

FICK. Hey, Ann?

DARLENE. You want a cup of coffee or something?

JOE. In a minute.

FRANNY. No, it's not my game.

DARLENE. I talked to Ann all afternoon.

FRANNY. Sorry, Rake.

JOE. She's a wild kid.

DARLENE. Kid, hell.

FICK. Hell.

ANN. Hell no, you aren't frostbit. It's not even cold out.

FICK. You sure?

FRANNY. It won't be real quick, I can tell you that right now.

FICK. 'Cause I can't tell.

TIG. I'll let you savor it a hour maybe.

KAY. How's business been?

JOHN. Not good, not bad. Coffee, Ann?

FRANNY. Or three. I could give you a ride you won't forget.

ANN. Why not.

TIG. You think so, huh?

JOE. She's nice, I like her.

DARLENE. So do I, really.

DOPEY. *(Turning his head around. To audience.)* Are you getting any of this?

FICK. Could I have a coffee?

JOHN. *(To Fick.)* Are you awake?

FRANNY. How long do you have to hang around your friends here?

FICK. Awake?

TIG. What friends?

RAKE. I don't believe it!

FRANNY. Believe anything, baby.

TIG. What can I tell you?

FICK. What is it, November?

DARLENE. I like her. I talked her leg off. *(Joe laughs.)*

FRANNY. Come on up, you springy son-of-a-bitch.

TIG. You better be all you claim.

ERNESTO. Want a party?

FRANNY. I'm not dressed for it. *(To Tig.)* I'll just bet you got action like a jack rabbit.

TIG. How much is it worth to find out?

FRANNY. *(As he and Tig start to leave.)* Well, we'll talk about it. Okay?

JOE. You want to go in?

DARLENE. Might as well. I've been in all day, though. *(Joe and Darlene enter the café.)*

RAKE. *(To Tig and Franny.)* Hey, you're gonna lose it, baby.

FRANNY. I never had it. *(The next four speeches are delivered rapidly over the above.)*

ERNESTO. You'll get split open, Franny!

RAKE. Rip him apart.

DOPEY. Give it to her.

ERNESTO. Make him cry for mercy, Tig.

TIG. I'll have him beggin' in five minutes.

FRANNY. Quit bragging and get to work. I'll see you guys later. *(Group laughs. The group moves back a few feet. Tig and Frannie exit. The Stranger should be standing where the last line of Franny's is spoken.)*

DOPEY. *(To audience.)* Wheeh! Jesus.

ANN. *(Leaving the café and joining the group.)* Did he do it? The son-of-a-bitch! Damn Franny.

RAKE. You got Sammy.

ANN. Damn Sam. I been trying to make Tig for a month.

ERNESTO. Don't tell Sammy.

ANN. Screw Sammy.

DOPEY. Franny'll end up like old Howie yet.

ANN. Poor old Howie. *(Darlene and Joe sit in a booth.)*

DOPEY. Poor old Howie. *(Group laughs.)*

RAKE. Son-of-a-bitch! *(Group laughs.)* Wire.... *(Laughs.)*

ANN. God, that's funny. It really is. *(During Ann's following speech the café is filled by the same people as in the beginning scene of the play. Black and orange crêpe-paper streamers are lowered very slowly in a typical crisscross Halloween decoration. A dime-store skeleton and a pumpkin should lower straight from the ceiling. The quartette is rehearsing the opening song in the back. To audience.)* There's this joke: I can't tell it. Not a joke joke, but like a private joke on this guy Howie from around here.

RAKE. *(Over, in background.)* Poor old Howie.

ANN. Like the devil gets his due, you understand. See, he's always around and for three or four dollars, I don't know how much, I never bothered to ask, but the guys around here would always pick up a few bucks from Howie. He's not an old guy either, I mean not all that old, but they'd step into a doorway or some dark place along the street or some rest-room, you follow me, and the guys would make about four or five bucks — a symbiotic kind of relationship — you know, the guys get the money and Howie gets, or derives, his benefit from it too: This is sounding vulgar as hell and I thought I could tell it clean. Well, anyway — Fuck. Howie gives them a quickie blow job in a subway john or some-where — Christ, we're all adult and know about that, I'd hope, by now, anyway. And this is very important to him. Like a junkie needs his shot in the arm. Well, poor Howie, God love him, never hurt anybody, was down in the Village and just out to see the sights, not approaching anyone or anything, at least no more than he could help; just walking around and some guys jump him. Figure him for a good rolling, and maybe they got a few dollars off the guy and left him pretty beaten up but that wouldn't be so bad for Howie, you know — and he made it to the hospital. Over to Saint Vincent's, see, and they gave him X rays and he's got his face knocked in and his teeth loosened; nothing really bad or serious or permanent, you understand. He'll be back in shape in about a month; but in the meantime he's got this broken jaw....

RAKE. Hey, Ann; come on.

ANN. So they wired his mouth shut! *(Group reaction. Ann laughs at her own joke.)*

DOPEY.   Poor bastard, Howie.

RAKE.   Poor Howie. *(Group laughs. Fick exits café. Ann reenters.)*

FICK.   *(As he passes Ann.)* Hey, Ann, you got — hey, you.... *(She is gone.)*

JUDY.   All right! Come on, come on. If we're going to get goin', get goin'; get that table out of the way, come on, line them up a little. *(They straighten the booths into rows. Blocking on these repeat scenes should be as the first time through exactly.)*

TIG.   *(Overlapping.)* What are you? Some kind of housewife, Judy?

JUDY.   *(To David.)* You're the housewife, aren't you, sweetheart?

DAVID.   You're the fishwife, Judy. Fishwife! Fish! Pheew!

FICK.   Hey, Dopey, you got a cigarette, huh?

DOPEY.   Somewhere.

BONNIE.   *(To David.)* You ought to be chased out of the neighborhood. Dirty up the neighborhood with a lot of fairy dust.

DAVID.   *(Not Franny, this time.)* Who you calling names, you truck driver?

BONNIE.   Who you queers think you are?

DAVID.   Who you callin' queer? George!

BOB.   Shut up, over there!

JOHN.   *(Not Tig.)* Come on, God.

TERRY.   All you queens.

DAVID.   *(To Terry.)* Why don't you shut up before I beat you over your head with your dildo?

TERRY.   You trying to say something?

DAVID.   Ah, your mother's a whore —

TERRY.   You trying to say something? *(Four children, three boys and a girl, enter the scene. They are dressed in regular clothes; they all have on Halloween masks. The boys wear comical masks; the girl a woman's mask. They carry big paper bags and go about saying "trick or treat." No one in the café pays the slightest attention to them. The scene is repeated as though they weren't there. All new material is ignored by the others.)*

JOHN.   Come on, now; keep it down.

TIM.   May I have a cup of tea, please? *(Carlo enters.)* Hi, Carlo. Over here.

CARLO.   *(Trying English.)* Hello. Correct? Yes, hello. Correct?

TIM.   *(With Spanish accent.)* Correct. Near enough. *(The next few lines will be over the repeat below, beginning with Bonnie's speech; but they should be loud and excited.)* Try the numbers, though. That's what you're working on.

CARLO.   Numbers. No. *(Quickly counts to ten as a joke — in Spanish.)*

TIM.   No. No. No. In English. In English. How you ever gonna learn anything?

ANN.   He'll never get it anyway.

CARLO.   Yes!

TIM.   Yes, he will. You wait.

BONNIE.   What the hell is this, fifty cents for one Coke; you think this is the Ritz?

JOHN.   There's a sign right there, fifty cents minimum at booths; if, you don't have it, don't sit there.

FICK.   *(On the corner, to Dopey.)* Hey, ain't we seen this once?

DOPEY.   It's important.

A CHILD.   Trick or treat!?

FICK.   They're new!

DOPEY.   Shut up, for Chris' sake.

BONNIE.   Screw it; I'm paying no fifty cents for one Coke.

KAY   *(To John.)* Toast with that.

BOB.   Fifty cents you can get a good high.

BONNIE.   Gimme a grilled cheese, hell, if I'm going to spend a fortune. One goddamned Coke.

KAY.   And a jack.

BONNIE.   Christ, you'd think this place was the Ritz!

DAVID.   *(To Bob.)* Come on up to my room. It won't kill you.

ANN.   It won't kill you, Bob.

STRANGER.   *(Enters and comes to Joe.)* Hi again.

JOE.   I don't know you.

BOB.   Knock it off.

DAVID.   Come on up with me, it won't hurt you.

BOB.   *(To Ann.)* How much scratch? Jack? Tonight?

ANN.   None of your damn business. Ask Sammy, you want to know.

JOHN.   You still keepin' that bum? What's he do with all that dough?

ANN.   He banks it. Or at least he'd better be banking it.

BOB. Yeah, he banks it with Cameron or Chuckles.

ANN. He don't truck with that junk. He'd better not; I'd crack him over the head. *(Dopey has turned to the audience as the stranger first spoke. Dopey's speech is over the scene in the café. He speaks to the audience, quite casually.)*

DOPEY. See, what happened, the whole thing — Joe's a nice guy; he really is, but you bum around and you bum around and you start to wonder just how the hell you're going to ever get out of it; and you think if you could get in a good position — if you could get in with Chuckles. See, there's a lot of dough being made around. And he figured he'd have some of it. But see, he really didn't like the idea, the risk, of pushing, so he wasn't tough enough for it. And it's as simple as that. And Chuckles is big. These guys are big, some of them. Those boys are about as powerful as anyone in the country, I guess, and you don't cross them is the thing. It isn't done. Everything would have been okay, but, see, Joe didn't know till a few days ago that he didn't want to go in with Chuckles. And Chuckles just naturally thought that Joe was holding out on him. Now for once he was patient. He sent a fellow to tell Joe to shape up. You saw that all right. And he tried to protect his investment. But even for once is a rare thing with Chuckles and Joe just didn't let him *know.* Now Chuckles is a big guy around here. He bleeds these guys around here. He can't have them see him made a fool of. And he gave Joe time. *(This last is almost screamed over the scene in the back.)*

FICK. *(To Dopey.)* He did, that's true. That's true as can be. He wouldn't do that for me.

DOPEY. *(Still to audience.)* So now they're gonna kill him.

FICK. Joe?

DOPEY. Yeah.

FICK. We ain't seen this, have we? *(Dopey shakes his head, quietly; mouths, "No." They turn toward the stage to watch.)*

STRANGER. *(This follows Ann's last line before Dopey's speech to the audience: some of it will be covered by the end of Dopey's speech. He takes a cattle syringe from his pocket.)* You ever see one of these?

JOE. What?

STRANGER. One of these?

JOE. A syringe? Christ, look at the size of it. What is it, a works

73

for elephants? *(He laughs.)*

STRANGER. For livestock. For cattle and pigs.

JOE. You don't use something like that. That's too fancy. You use a works. An eye dropper, a piece of dollar.* A needle.

TIM. *(To Carlo.)* One, two, three, four, five.

STRANGER. You do, huh?

CARLO. No. No.

TIM. Slow then. One. Come on. One.

A CHILD. Trick or treat.

JOHN. Get out of here, you kids, go on.

STRANGER. You do, huh?

JOE. They do. Why do you show me that?

ANN. *(To Tim.)* He'll never get it.

CARLO. One!

TIM. *(Not too loudly.)* Bravo.

JOE. *(Over.)* I've got no use for it.

DARLENE. *(To Joe.)* What's wrong?

TIM. Two. Come on.

JOE. *(To Darlene.)* Nothing.

STRANGER. Chuckles wanted you to know what hit you. Understand? That's a four-inch reach. You don't screw Chuckles. Understand?

JOE. *(Stands. To Stranger.)* I got something to tell him.

DARLENE. What? What is it?

JOE. No! Come on.

JOHN. *(To the Children.)* Go on, scram. Get out of here. Scram out of here. Go on! *(Dim on café. Spot on Joe and Stranger. Stranger reaches back and stabs Joe underhanded in the heart.)*

BOB. God!

TERRY. Jesus!

DARLENE. *(Over.)* No! *(Simultaneously, the Children run out with the paper sacks flapping over their heads. They are screaming and yelling joyously. They split and two go one way, two another. They circle around the café and enter from the back and run through again. Lights up on café.)*

---

* A junkie seldom uses a syringe. He uses an eye-dropper, attached to a surgical needle with a thin piece of paper rolled around the needle, serving as a gasket. For paper they often use a thin strip torn from the edge of a dollar bill.

THE SCENE IS REPEATED.

JOHN.   Go on, scram. Get out of here. Scram out of here. Go on!
(Dim on café. Spot on Joe and Stranger. The Stranger stabs Joe as before.)
BOB.   God!
TERRY.   Jesus!
DARLENE.   *(Over.)* No! *(The Children run out and circle the café as before. Lights up on café.)*

THE SCENE IS REPEATED.

JOHN.   Go on, scram. Get out of here. Scram out of here. Go on!
(Dim on café. Spot on Joe and Stranger. The Stranger stabs Joe.)
BOB.   God!
TERRY.   Jesus! *(The Children run through the café.)*
JOE.   *(Pulls a number of white packets from his pockets and spills them all over the stage in front of him.)* I don't want them. I don't want it! Take them! Take them back! I don't want them! *(The Children split in twos and run off screaming.)*
DARLENE.   *(Over screaming.)* No, no, no, no! *(The Stranger walks off. Joe falls among Bob, Terry, Ann, Carlo, and Tim. Joe is taken behind the counter, away, out of sight of the audience. Not hidden, but removed from audience's sight. There is a time lapse. No one mentions the stabbing. Darlene sits through this scene without comment or without looking up.)*
TIG.   *(Instantly, as soon as Joe falls. Frank is behind the counter now.)* What the hell are you talking about....
FRANK.   Why don't you stop coming in here, you don't —
TIG.   What the hell, you're trying to screw —
FRANK.   *(Cutting in.)* Get on out now.
TIG.   You trying to cheat me outta four bucks, baby, you can't pull —
FRANK.   I never cheat you outta nothing.
TERRY.   *(Over, to David.)* You queers just sit down, take it easy.
TIG.   I gave you a five, a five, you son of —
FRANK.   You get on out of here.
TIG.   You want to step outside? You want to step out from behind that counter, baby? You watch it, Frank.
JOHN.   *(Cutting in.)* Come on, Tig, give up, go on out.
FRANK.   Get out of this place.
TIM.   Try again.
ANN.   He's not gonna get it, I know.

CARLO.   Yes.

TIG.   Ah, come on, I gave him a five, man, you know what he's trying.

JOHN.   Come on, go on, Tig.

CARLO.   One.

JOHN.   Come on, go on, Tig.

TIG.   *(Leaving.)* You wait, Frank; you'll get yours, buddy.

FRANK.   *(After Tig has gone.)* Get on out of here, bum!

TIG.   *(Yelling back heatedly.)* All right, now, goddamnit I'm out, you just shut your mouth, Frank; you stupid bastard. Buddy, you're really gonna get it one day, Frank, and I want to be there to watch it. You're gonna get your head split open, dumb bastard.

FICK.   *(Very clearly during the fray, to Dopey, who ignores the question.)* Hey, where's Joe?

RUST.   *(Running in to café.)* Hey, they got Jerry Joe in the can!

BOB.   Jerry the fairy?

DAVID.   You watch who you're calling names.

RUST.   He tried to put the make on a cop.

BOB.   They gonna book him?

RUST.   Whatta you mean? He tried to put the make on a cop. Hell, yes, they'll book him. He had eight bombinos on him! Man, are they hot for that stuff. *(General crowd reaction.)*

TIM.   She's right, you'll never learn.

CARLO.   *Si* — no, yes! I will.

TIM.   Say, "Yes, I will."

CARLO.   Yes, I will. *(General crowd murmur to themselves during this.)*

TIM.   You're getting the wrong damn accent. Just repeat it. Take it slow. You'll learn.

ANN.   Not a chance, Timmy. He's never learned anything.

TIM.   He will. One.

CARLO.   *(Repeating rapidly.)* One.

TIM.   Two.

CARLO.   Two.

TIM.   Three.

CARLO.   Three.

TIM.   Four.

CARLO.   Four.

TIM.   Five.

CARLO.   Fife.

TIM.   Five, Carlo; five, five!

CARLO.   *(Overlapping.)* Yes, I know. Five.

TIM.   Good, six.

CARLO.   Six. *(On "six" the quartette enters with a downbeat as at the beginning, singing the first five bars of the rock'n'roll song.)*

TIM.   Come on!

ANN.   *(Loudly breaking it up.)* No. Stop it! No, stop it. You can't do it that way. It isn't right. *(They stop, wander off for a retake. Apologetically.)* It's just not it, you know — not right. *(During Ann's speech Tim and Carlo have begun counting again. They reach "seven" and the quartette returns as before with as much of the song. Ann and John shout them down. Everyone is wandering about aimlessly. To quartette.)* No, come on. Stop it.

TERRY.   *(To quartette.)* Knock it off — come on.

ANN.   *(To John.)* It's just not the way to end it. *(Quartette exits as before.)*

JOHN.   I *know.* Try to tell them something. God. *(Tim and Carlo have started over again. Dopey, Rake, and Bob have run up to stop the quartette.)*

TIM.   Four.

CARLO.   Four.

TIM.   Five.

CARLO.   Five.

TIM.   Good, six.

CARLO.   Six.

TIM.   Seven.

CARLO.   Seven.

TIM.   Eight.

CARLO.   Eight.

TIM.   Nine.

CARLO.   Nine.

TIM.   Ten.

CARLO.   Ten.

TIM.   Good! *(At "ten" Dopey, Rake, and Bob begin their round, D. C. This time not as a round, but all singing softly and liltingly.)*

DOPEY, RAKE AND BOB.
>THEY LAUGH AND JAB
>CAVORT AND JUMP
>AND JOKE AND GAB
>AND GRIND AND BUMP.
>
>THEY FLIP A KNIFE
>AND TOSS A COIN
>AND SPEND THEIR LIFE
>AND SCRATCH THEIR GROIN.
>
>THEY PANTOMIME
>A STANDING SCREW
>AND PASS THE TIME
>WITH NOUGHT TO DO.
>
>THEY SWING, THEY SWAY
>THIS CHEERFUL CREW,
>WITH NOUGHT TO SAY
>AND NOUGHT TO DO.

(The cast hums the tune very softly. During the song the crêpe-paper and Halloween decorations ascend slowly. Everyone in the café picks up the "set" as before and slowly walks the set back toward its original position. Babe walks, as before, beside the others, not carrying the set. The lights dim slowly at the beginning of Dopey, Rake, and Bob's song.)

FICK.   *(Over the singing, cued by Tim's "Good!" He is wandering about the stage as at the beginning.)* Hey, buddy, hey, fellow ... hey, you got a cigarette on you? Hey ... Hey, Ann? Uh, cold, huh? Uh, Dopey, you got.... Hey.... Hey.... *(The song has finished. Several continue to hum. Everyone sets the "set" back in its original place and takes a position similar to the beginning, only Fick is sitting at a table and Darlene and Ann are at the counter, backs to audience. The lights hold at about half.)*

RAKE   *(To no one, looking at no one.)* You travel around, I mean a hustler travels around....

DOPEY.   *(To no one, to himself.)* And they cut down, through one century to the one before that, and the one before that....

FICK.   *(At the booth, to himself.)* You know what I mean? You know what I mean?... You know what I mean?... I mean....

DARLENE.   *(To Ann, very slow, tired, after a kind of sigh.)* And, I don't know. Everyone was so tired and so down, and I thought, Christ, aren't we even moving? You know? *(The lights have faded out. Curtain.)*

PROPERTY LIST

Change (money) (TIG, FRANK)
Restaurant checks (BONNIE, ANN, ERNESTO)
Money (ANN, ERNESTO)
Coffee
Coffee cups
Milk
Cigarettes (DARLENE, JOE, ANN)
Lighter or matches (JOE)
Matches (DARLENE)
Package of cigarettes (DARLENE)
Towel (DARLENE)
Cigarette (TIG)
Newspaper (FRANK)
Belt (JOE)
Paper bags (CHILDREN)
Cattle syringe (STRANGER)
White packets (JOE)